AF335132

THE PROPHET JOEL

and the

DAY OF THE LORD

By

WALTER K. PRICE

MOODY PRESS

CHICAGO

Library of Congress Cataloging in Publication Data

Price, Walter K.
    The Prophet Joel and the day of the Lord.
    Includes bibliographical references.
    1. Bible. O.T. Joel—Criticism, interpretation, etc.
2. Day of Jehovah. I. Title.

BS1575.2.P74   224'.7'066   76-23253

ISBN 0-8024-6904-3

CONTENTS

FOREWORD

When the apostle Peter on the day of Pentecost introduced his message by quoting Joel 2:28-32, he recognized the major role of Joel as a prophet of the end time. Peter chided his generation for being unacquainted with Joel, and his criticism probably extends to our modern generation.

Joel the prophet made the important contribution of discussing at length the Day of the Lord, the comprehensive period that embraces end-time events, including the millennial reign of Christ. The study of Joel is essential to understanding the prophetic program and to reaching a proper interpretation of the New Testament passages dealing with this prophesied period.

A study of the Day of the Lord is an important introduction to the subject of the millennial reign of Christ as it is presented in the Old and New Testaments. It is also the key to understanding the relationship of the rapture to end-time events. Even worthy scholars have been guilty of ignoring what the Old Testament teaches about the Day of the Lord.

This exposition of Joel by one who is skilled in dealing with prophetic Scriptures should do much to correct the ignorance and misapprehension which has attended many references to the Day of the Lord in modern literature. As the author, Walter K. Price, points out in his own inimitable style, the Day of the Lord includes not only the glorious reign of Christ on earth for a thousand years, but the events of the Great Tribulation which will precede it. On the basis of the description of the Day of the Lord in Joel, Price understands

1 Thessalonians 5 and 2 Thessalonians 2 to support the pre-Tribulation rapture of the Church.

Although the minor prophets are not always high in reader interest, students of this exposition of the prophet Joel will find the study fascinating, challenging, and helpful.

JOHN F. WALVOORD

1

THE ANNOUNCEMENT OF THE DAY OF THE LORD
Joel 1:1

Some of England's greatest monarchs have been women. Queen Victoria ruled for thirty-six years. She could boast of the longest reign in English history before she died in 1901. The term *Victorian Era* suggests that this queen personified her times. She was immensely popular. When Queen Elizabeth I came to the throne in 1558, England was in great trouble, filled with religious strife, deeply in debt, and unable to terminate the wars with France. It was Elizabeth who guided England through these troubled times and moored her to her greatest glory. The Elizabethan Age is no less famous than is the Victorian Era.

Israel was not so fortunate.

Only one queen ever sat upon the throne of David, and she was a usurper. She was certainly no Golda Meir, for her reign was a disaster. Athaliah was her name, and she ruled in Judah between 842 and 836 B.C.

Athaliah, the daughter of Ahab and his notorious wife, Jezebel, inherited all of her mother's evil qualities. Athaliah's son had been ruling as king in Judah, but the throne of the Southern Kingdom became vacant when he was mowed down in ambush by Jehu while on his way to Jezreel. Hearing of her son's murder, Athaliah wasted no time. She voided the claim of her grandchildren to the throne of Judah by having them slain. With all of the seed royal destroyed—or so she thought—she usurped the throne herself and established a reign which was to cause the kingdom of Judah to groan for the next six years. Baalism, the coerced worship of a pagan god, marked the uneasy reign of Queen Athaliah. Then one day her guards reported to her that a great crowd was gathering in the sacred sanctuary. Commanding a chariot to be made ready, she rode over to the Temple to investigate.

The throng fell back before her royal presence and, as the gathering parted, Athaliah saw a small boy standing by the sacred pillar in the Temple. Anointing oil glistened upon his brow, giving evidence of what had just taken place. The priests had but a few moments before declared him sovereign, the king of Judah. A crown was upon his head. The people clapped their hands and cried, "Long live the king!" And so he would, for Joash, who was seven years old at this time, reigned for the next forty years in Jerusalem.

The queen did not recognize the boy, but he was her own grandson. He had escaped her vengeance a few years before during her terrible purge of the other heirs to the throne. Since then he had been hidden in the Temple. During all that time the priests had protected Joash and had given him instructions in the office of king in anticipation of this, his coronation day. During those years, the preservation of the royal line of David was invested in a single thread—the life of this child.

"Treason! Treason!" screamed the outraged queen when she realized what was happening. But the crowd, intimidated by her entrance, no longer was awed by her theatrical performance. Suddenly the people turned upon her. Jehoiada, the high priest, ordered her execution. She was taken to the Kidron Valley, says Josephus, and there slain, although the Scripture says she was killed in "the horses' entry to the king's house" (2 Ki 11:16). Joash's right to the throne was now cleared. This occurred in approximately 836 B.C. For the next few years Judah would have a minor king, and the land would be ruled by Jehoiada, the high priest, acting as king regent. He would instruct the boy king during those early days of his minority, just as William Marshal, Earl of Pembroke, acted as regent in England when nine-year-old Henry III assumed the throne upon the death of his father, King John, in 1216.

The prophet Joel probably witnessed these events in Jerusalem.

However, there are students of the book of Joel who would disagree with this, for many modern critics tend to date Joel's prophecy much later. It is popular to fix a time for Joel after the Exile and assign to his ministry a slot in the Persian period, at about 400 B.C. when Jerusalem was ruled by the high priests. Some date Joel's book even later than this, placing it in the Greek period, at about 200 B.C. The reason why they assume that Joel was written later is because he neither mentioned a king of Judah nor did he make allusion to Israel's great preexilic enemies, Syria, Assyria, and Babylon. Furthermore, many critics of his book believe that Joel made extensive use of material found in the books of the other writing prophets, suggesting that he lived much later than they.

It was a characteristic of many preexilic prophets to indicate the king in whose reign they ministered the word of God. Joel mentioned no king. This strengthens the critics' position that he wrote after the Exile, when Jerusalem was under the administration of the high priests during the Persian period. However, the fact that Joash was a small boy and that the land was ruled by a regent during this era could also account for the prophet's failure to speak about a king.

As for the great enemies of Israel—Syria, Assyria, and Babylon—all three could have long since passed off the scene of Near Eastern history. If this is the case, then we are bound to concede a very late date for the book of Joel. However,

these enemy nations might not have arisen as yet to threaten
Judah. Syria, Assyria, and Babylon could still have been in
the wings, preparing to assert their respective claim over
Israel. If we assign an early date for Joel's prophecy, as early
as the ninth-century reign of King Joash, then we are assum-
ing that Israel's three great preexilic enemies had not arisen
yet, and this is why Joel made no mention of them.

Many students of this book believe that the scales were
tipped in the direction of an early date by the Jews who made
up the canon of the Hebrew Bible. These Jewish compilers
placed the prophecy of Joel between Hosea and Amos, where
it remains today in our Old Testament. Both Hosea and
Amos prophesied early, during the Assyrian period (eighth
century B.C.), which suggests that the Jewish compilers of
the canon felt that Joel belonged among the very earliest of
the writing prophets of Israel.

What difference does it make?

Does it really matter if Joel was written early, in the ninth
century B.C., or much later, after the Exile?

If we assume that Joel was written later than the Babylonian Exile, then this affects the book's originality, perhaps
even the integrity of his prophecy, for many things in his
book are also in Isaiah, Amos, Micah, Nahum, Zephaniah,
Obadiah, Ezekiel, and Malachi. In fact, Professor Driver lists
sixteen literary parallels between the material in Joel and
that found in the other prophets.[1] Horton says, "In seventy-
two verses there are twenty of these literary parallels." He
declares that if we "place the book at the end, and not at the
beginning, of the line of the prophets, we become aware how
curiously it echoes all of them, and even quotes from many
of them, from Amos to Malachi."[2] Therefore, if Joel wrote
later, there is no doubt but that he lifted much of his material from his predecessors and incorporated it into his book.
He was guilty of plagiarizing Jewish eschatology, whose content was originated by other writers. He purloined their

ideas, repeating them in his own book and sometimes using their exact words. If he is the last of the canonical prophets, then Joel trailed all of his predecessors, not only in time but also in the originality of his content.

There is an alternative, for most critics agree that if Joel's prophecy was not later than the Exile, then it was very early. If Joel wrote late, then he was not very original. But if he wrote early, in the ninth century B.C., then his book stands at the fountainhead of Hebrew predictive prophecy. His book inaugurated biblical apocalyptic writing as a form of revelation. He was the first to use a current crisis as the framework for forecasting the future, and 68 percent of his prophecy is predictive, according to Professor Payne.[3]

Given an early date for Joel, we are therefore dealing with a vital source of Great Tribulation prophecy, for Joel is to be credited with originating the idea of the Day of the Lord upon Israel and the nations. Eiselen says that if one accepts the early date for Joel, then his book becomes "a kind of prophetic chart."[4]

Therefore, Joel is a basic text for all students of predictive prophecy, for he introduced the idea of the Day of the Lord. This day becomes the frame of reference in the Lord's climactic program for *Israel* and the *nations*. It also gives rise to another prophetic category—the day of Christ—in which God deals terminally with a third group, the *Church*.

Dr. Sampey suggests that it was around 830 B.C.,[5] during the reign of Joash, when the devastating plague of locusts scourged the land of Judah. This was followed by a severe drought which threatened famine. Joel, whose name affirms that "Yahweh is God," saw the hand of God in this destructive pestilence. Joel believed that this could be the Day of the Lord upon Israel, unless the people changed their minds. He proclaimed this sole remedy for the people's plight: repentance! As a result of his preaching, that was exactly what the people did. The judgment of the Day of the Lord was averted, and in its place the people were promised blessings from God. Nevertheless, this does not mean that an apocalyptic Day of the Lord will never come, for it will. But when it does come, it will be directed against the nations who have conspired to devastate Israel just as the locusts did. Israel will also be involved in the final Day of the Lord, but not in a strictly punitive way. While the nations find no escape from the judgment of that day, a faithful remnant in Israel will escape. It is this remnant who will repent and accept the Lord Jesus as Messiah. It is they who will become the subjects of the Messianic Kingdom.

The format of Joel, in which he wove the contemporary plague of locusts and the anticipated Day of the Lord together, is masterfully done in the literature of his book. He joined together current events and prophecy—history and prediction—in an exciting account of a horrible plague, drought, and famine. All of these are recognized ingredients in apocalyptic revelation. Therefore Joel's oracles combine narrative and prediction in the context of an unprecedented plague of locusts which afflicted Judah in the prophet's own day.

The book of Joel can be divided into two parts.

First, Joel depicted a national disaster in the form of a ravaging locust plague. He issued several calls to the people to repent, and apparently a nationwide repentance resulted (1:2—2:18). Though this national repentance was not recorded, it probably took place between verses 17 and 18 of chapter 2.

In this initial section the prophet pictured the advent of the locusts (1:2-14). No plague in memory had been so severe (1:2). Its thoroughness would be remembered and told to future generations (1:3-4). As a result of this desolation, the drunkards (1:5-7), the priests (1:8-9), and the farmers (1:10-12) were called upon to lament their plight. Joel then issued his first call to repentance (1:13-14).

All of Judah's agony was but a harbinger of the coming Day of the Lord (1:15—2:11). Its shadow could be seen in the drought (1:15-20) which accompanied the insect holocaust. However, it was the locust intrusion itself which was the most graphic precursor of the Day of the Lord (2:1-11). Although they were insects, their coming was like a storm (2:2). They were like a fire, for the land was an Eden before them but became a desolate wilderness after they had passed over it (2:3). They were like horses, for the sound of their arrival was as the whir of chariots (2:4-5). They reminded the prophet of an advancing infantry (2:6-10). Joel indicated his belief that this pillage could be the Day of the Lord (2:11).

The second call to repentance was heard (2:12-17). Joel admonished both individual (2:12-14) and national (2:15-17) repentance upon Judah.

An elapse of time in which the people actually carried out the prophet's admonition must be assumed between 2:17 and 2:18. They repented, and the Day of the Lord upon Israel was averted.

The second major division of the prophecy of Joel concerns the promised blessings upon Judah as a result of her repentance, plus the Day of the Lord which would now come upon Israel's enemies, the nations (2:18—3:21).

The blessings which Israel would receive were both present and future. First, there would be immediate blessings as a result of Judah's repentance (2:18-27). The northern army, the locusts, would be removed (2:18-20), and the land would be restored to fertility and to productivity (2:21-27).

Second, there also would be future blessings (2:28—3:21). The Holy Spirit would be poured out upon all flesh (2:28-29). Then signs and wonders would immediately precede the coming Day of the Lord (2:30-31). However, this need not affect Israel, for, even in the last days, whosoever among the Jews of that day shall call upon the name of the Lord shall be saved (2:32). The Day of the Lord, which could have fallen upon Israel via the locust holocaust if the people had not repented, will fall upon the nations. The reason is that the nations, in relentless and unrepentant hostility, have exploited the covenant people of God (3:1-17). Finally, Israel's ultimate blessing will come when the long-awaited golden age is ushered in (3:18-21).

The Day of the Lord is the day in which God will invade human history in a spectacular way. God has always projected Himself into human history in various ways, the incarnation being the most outstanding example. But Christ's birth was a veiled foray into the course of human affairs. Only those who were spiritually sensitive were aware of His advent. Only they realized that God through Jesus had, in this segment of history, become man. In contrast, the Day of the Lord will be a sensational and dramatic intrusion of God into the human pageant.

Will this incursion of God into human history via the Day of the Lord be a day of judgment or a day of blessing or both?

Unlike their neighbors in the ancient world, especially the Greeks and the Romans, Israel looked not backward but forward to their golden age. It lay in a future which would provide the crown and climax of the history of Israel.

This golden age will be ushered in by the Day of the Lord, said Joel. However, the prophet Amos warned that the Day of the Lord will also be a day of judgment (5:18-20). The people of Amos's day were overly impressed with the prospects of blessings in the Day of the Lord. Amos warned that the day would be "darkness, and not light."

Here then are both elements in the Day of the Lord. It will feature a universal judgment upon all the nations. Israel nationally will not escape the terrors of that day. However, individuals in Israel may escape by calling upon the name of the Lord (Joel 2:32). For those who do, this day of wrath will be followed by a time of great glory which will fill the earth during the Messianic age.

Professor Rowley says,

> The book of Joel presents this aspect of the Day of the Lord, which it too describes as "a day of darkness and gloom, a day of cloud and thundercloud." But it makes it clear that beyond the judgment in which all that was alien to God's will should be consumed there would be a new glory and light. "It shall come to pass afterward, that I will pour out my spirit upon all flesh. . . . And it shall come to pass that everyone who calls on the name of Yahweh shall be delivered; for in mount Zion and in Jerusalem there shall be those who escape, as Yahweh hath said, and among the survivors those whom Yahweh calls." In the section of the book of Isaiah which is most closely akin to apocalyptic writing we find a similar idea of judgment followed by a Golden Age. "The earth shall stagger like a drunken man, and shall sway to and fro like a hut. . . . And it shall come to pass in that day, that Yahweh will punish the host of the height on high, and the kings of the earth on the earth." Yet following the judgment we find "and it shall be said in that day, Lo, this is our God; we have waited for him, and he will save us: this is Yahweh; we have waited for him, let us be glad and rejoice in his salvation." The same pattern is found in the book of Daniel, where the thought of a general judgment on the nations introduces the promise of the inauguration of the enduring kingdom of the saints of the Most High.[6]

This indicates that the Day of the Lord can be confined neither to a twenty-four-hour period nor to a single event such as the second coming of Christ, nor to a single concept—judgment or blessing—for both will be a part of that day. The Day of the Lord covers all of God's intervention into history during the last days, especially as that intervention has to do with Israel and the nations who are the prime subjects of the Day of the Lord. Therefore the Day of the Lord, to use New Testament concepts, involves the Great Tribulation period, the Battle of Armageddon, the second coming of Christ, and the millennial reign of Jesus. All of these events are a part of that day and they include both judgment and blessing. But no one of them constitutes the day, for the day is made up of the whole program of God for Israel and the nations during the end time.

Therefore the Day of the Lord is an extended period of time covering a number of events scheduled to transpire during the last days which issue in judgment for apostate Israel and the nations, as well as in blessing for the faithful remnant in Israel who accept Jesus as Messiah. The Day of the Lord also has an extended emphasis, for both Israel and the nations are its subjects.

What are the implications of the Day of the Lord for the Church, the Body of Christ?

Since the Day of the Lord is designed for Israel and the nations and not for the Church, the Church will be taken out of the world before the Day of the Lord arrives. The New Testament uses a special term for the rapture of the Church which places it in contrast to the Day of the Lord. The Church anticipates the day of Christ (1 Co 1:8; 5:5; 2 Co 1:14; Phil 1:6, 10; 2:16; 2 Th 2:2-3*). This term, found mostly in Paul's epistles, refers exclusively to the Church. This means that the Church looks for the day of Christ but not for the Day of the Lord, since the Church does not go through the Tribulation.

The Church escapes the Day of the Lord, for that day is designed to bring Israel to repentance or to judgment. It is also designed to punish the nations. The prophecy of Joel affirms this. But the Church, having already repented and needing no further judgment than that which the Lord Jesus

---

*Although the term "the day of the Lord" is used in 2 Th 2:2, it refers there to "the day of Christ" rather than to the Old Testament Day of the Lord which will come upon Israel and the nations.

Christ took upon the cross, has no further involvement in the Day of the Lord. The Church awaits only the day of Christ, the rapture.

The Day of the Lord and the day of Christ are not distinctive periods. Rather, they seem to involve only a difference in emphasis. The day of Christ has to do with the Church, while the Day of the Lord focuses upon Israel and the nations. The day of Christ will begin at the rapture (1 Th 4:16-17) and run its course during the Tribulation period. So will the Day of the Lord. But their locations will differ. The day of Christ will focus upon the Church in the air. It will include the rapture, the judgment seat of Christ where rewards will be given to the saints (2 Co 5:10), and the marriage supper of the Lamb (Rev 19:6-9). The Day of the Lord focuses upon Israel and the nations during the Tribulation period (Rev 11-18), which runs its course upon earth concurrent with when the Church is in the air.

Since the times of the Gentiles will come to a close at the Battle of Armageddon (Rev 16:13-16), at that point the nations will drop from view in the Day of the Lord. During the Messianic age, which will follow the second advent of the Lord Jesus Christ, Israel alone will occupy the divine spotlight, along with the Church, of course, which will return to earth at the second coming (Mt 24:31-36). Therefore the day of Christ and the Day of the Lord will merge in the Messianic age where both Israel and the Church will participate in the millennial blessings during the Messianic reign of Jesus (Rev 21:1—22:5).

Therefore the day of Christ will take the Church out of the world, involving it in a judgment which will determine individual rewards, and the marriage supper of the Lamb. This will take place in the air while the Day of the Lord runs its course upon the earth. On earth, the Day of the Lord will focus upon Israel and the nations, bringing them to judgment during the Great Tribulation period. The judgment of apostate Israel and the nations will climax at the second coming of Christ. Apostate Israel will be judged for her capitulation to the beast. They will have worshiped him as god and will have forsaken Yahweh, the covenant God of their fathers. At this point in the prophetic program of God, the nations will be judged and drop from history. The Day of the Lord—no longer a day of judgment, but one of blessing—will continue upon Israel. The faithful remnant among the Jews, those who will not have received the mark of the beast (Rev 13:1-17) indicating that they refused to worship him as god, will then accept the Lord Jesus Christ as Messiah and Saviour. They will enter the golden age over which the Messiah, the Lord Jesus, will reign. The Church will also be in the Millennium (Rev 20:1-6). Therefore the day of Christ and the Day of the Lord will merge in the Messianic era as both Israel and the Church bask in the blessings of that day.

2

THE ANTICIPATION OF THE DAY OF THE LORD

Joel 1:2-12, 15-20; 2:1-11

OVER A HUNDRED YEARS AGO Dr. W. M. Thomson served as a missionary in Palestine. As a result of living there, he wrote an account of the manners, customs, climate, and scenery of the Holy Land. Even today his book remains a standard reference work. Thomson lived through an incursion of locusts much like that of Joel's day. He tells about the plague of 1845:

> For several days previous to the first of June we had heard that millions of young locusts were on their march up the valley toward our village, and at length I was told that they had reached the lower part of it. Summoning all the people I could collect, we went to meet and attack them, hoping to stop their progress altogether, or at least to turn aside the line of their march. Never shall I lose the impression produced by the first view of them. I had often passed through clouds of flying locusts, and they always struck my imagination with a sort of vague terror; but these we now confronted were without wings, and about the size of full-grown grasshoppers, which they closely resembled in appearance and behaviour. But their number was astounding; the whole face of the mountain was black with them. On they came like a living deluge. We dug trenches, and kindled fires, and beat, and burned to death heaps upon heaps, but

the effort was utterly useless. Wave after wave rolled up the mountain side, and poured over rocks, walls, ditches, and hedges, those behind covering up and bridging over the masses already killed. After a long and fatiguing contest, I descended the mountain to examine the depth of the column, but I could not see the end of it. Wearied with my hard walk over the living deluge, I returned, and gave over the vain effort to stop its progress.

By the next morning the head of the column had reached my garden, and, hiring eight or ten people, I resolved to rescue at least my vegetables and flowers. During this day we succeeded by fire, and by beating them off the walls with brushes and branches, in keeping our little garden tolerably clear of them; but it was perfectly appalling to watch this animated river as it flowed up the road and ascended the hill above my house. At length, worn out with incessant skirmishing, I gave up the battle. Carrying the pots into the parlor, and covering up what else I could, I surrendered the remainder to the conquerors. For four days they continued to pass on toward the east, and finally only a few stragglers of the mighty hosts were left behind. . . . In their march they devour every green thing, and with wonderful expedition. A large vineyard and garden adjoining mine was green as a meadow in the morning, but long before night it was naked and bare as a newly-plowed field or dusty road. The noise made in marching and foraging was like that of a heavy shower on a distant forest. . . . I saw under my own eye not only a large vineyard loaded with young grapes, but whole fields of corn disappear as if by magic. . . . When the head of the mighty column came in contact with the palace of the Emeer Asaad in Abeih, they did not take the trouble to wheel round the corners, but climbed the wall like man of war, and marched over the top of it; so, when they reached the house of Dr. Van Dyck, in spite of all his efforts to prevent it, a living stream rolled right over the roof.[1]

Joel believed that such a locust plague in his day indicated that the Day of the Lord was near for Israel. If the people did not repent, it would surely come. Only national repentance could avert this day of certain judgment.

The elements involved in Joel's forecast of the Day of the Lord—his description of the locust plague and the interpretation of that plague—are found in Joel 1:2-12, 15-20; 2:1-11.

A description of the plague is given in detail in 1:2-20.

Joel presented the ravaging of the locusts by calling upon three groups to lament—the drunkards, the priests, and the farmers (1:5-12). As the prophet made reference to each group, he revealed the intensity of the plague.

First, the farmers were addressed (1:11-12). Because of the plague and the drought, "the harvest of the field is perished. The vine is withered, and the fig-tree languisheth; the pomegranate-tree, the palm-tree also, and the apple-tree, even all the trees of the field are withered." This catastrophe should have caused great consternation among the farmers whose plight Joel urged them to lament. When the extent of their loss would be finally realized, they would turn pale in the face of their tragedy.

In the United States presidential election of 1844, Henry Clay of Kentucky, the Whig candidate, opposed James K. Polk of Tennessee. Clay had run before, in 1824, when he was defeated by John Quincy Adams. The election was held on November 4, 5, and 6. Communications were slow in those days, so the outcome of the election was not known for many days. The November 13, 1844, *The Lexington Observer and Reporter* announced that the results of the election hinged on the returns from the state of New York. In a few more days news reached Lexington, Clay's hometown, that Polk had carried the Empire State. Henry Clay had lost the election.

How did he receive the news of his defeat?

The New York mail was due in Lexington on the 10 P.M. stagecoach. Mrs. Robert S. Todd, Abraham Lincoln's mother-

in-law, was present at the gathering where Clay received the
news. She wrote about the events of that night to her daughter:

> As the hour approached for the arrival of the mail, I saw
> several gentlemen quietly leave the room, and knowing their
> errand, I eagerly watched for their return. As soon as they
> came in the room I knew by the expression on each counte-
> nance that New York had gone Democratic. The bearers of
> the news consulted together a moment, then one of them
> advanced to Mr. Clay who was standing in the center of the
> group, of which your father was one, and handed him a pa-
> per. Although I was sure of the news it contained, I watched
> Mr. Clay's face for confirmation of the evil tidings. He
> opened the paper and as he read the death knell of his po-
> litical hopes and life-long ambition, I saw a distinct blue
> shade begin at the roots of his hair, pass slowly over his face
> like a cloud and then disappear. He stood for a moment as
> if frozen.[2]

Henry Clay blanched visibly at the news of political tragedy. Joel admonished his hearers, the farmers, to do the
same! "Turn pale," said the prophet to these farmers, at the
news of the locust plague. The American Standard Version
renders it, "Be confounded, O ye husbandmen" (1:11). The
Hebrew word suggests an intense disappointment manifesting
itself in a change of color, exactly what Henry Clay experienced. Keil actually translates it, "Turn pale, ye husbandmen."[3]

Joel not only called upon the farmers to "turn pale" because the harvest of the field had perished, but he urged them
to wail, along with the priests and the drunkards, over their
common tragedy.

Besides the farmers, the drunkards were also to weep and
wail (1:5-7). They were to awake from their intoxicated
sleep, for there was no more wine available. The locusts had

destroyed the vines and, along with them, the possibility of any sweet wine or "new wine."

The locusts which caused such destruction were "without number." This was no exaggeration. In 1888 a swarm of locusts which was estimated to extend for two thousand square miles passed over the Red Sea area. Estimating that each locust weighed one-sixteenth of an ounce, the weight of the swarm was calculated to be 42,850 million tons.[4]

The drunkards were to lament the coming of the locusts because they had "laid my vine waste, and barked my fig-tree: he hath made it clean bare, and cast it away: the branches thereof are made white" (1:7). Thomson says,

> The references to the habits and behaviour of the locusts in the Bible are very striking and accurate. . . . These locusts at once strip the vines of every leaf and cluster of grapes, and of every green twig. I also saw many large fig orchards "clean bare," not a leaf remaining; and as the bark of the fig-tree is of a silvery whiteness, the whole orchard thus rifled of their green veils, spread abroad their branches "made white" in melancholy nakedness to the burning sun.[5]

How untenable is the drunkard's security. It is invested in a grape which an insect can destroy, sending the drunkard into chaos.

Third, the priests were included in the lamentation (1:8-10). Because meal offerings and drink offerings were cut off from the house of the Lord, the priests, the Lord's ministers, mourned.

Joel used a feminine singular verb when he directed the priests to "lament like a virgin girded with sackcloth for the husband of her youth" (1:8). What the joys of marriage could have meant to this young widow, the Temple sacrifices and libations meant to the priests. But these offerings had ceased because the locusts had destroyed the grain for the meal offering and the grapes for the drink offering. "The field is laid waste, the land mourneth; for grain is destroyed, the new wine is dried up, the oil languisheth" (1:10).

The ravaging of the locusts caused the farmer and the drunkard to suffer. Food for the hungry could not be found. The drunkard, who could get no more drink, suffered the pangs of his unquenched thirst. However, their suffering was physical. Joel indicated the more subtle suffering of the priests, for they were denied the Levitical offerings which, in those days, were fundamental to the worship of the God of Israel. The Levitical offerings ceased, and the Temple services were, for the moment, shut down because there was no more grain or wine for the major offerings.

The Jews would suffer this same anguish many times in the years that lay ahead.

In 168 B.C. Antiochus IV Epiphanes stripped the Temple of all of its vessels and stopped the sacrifices.

> Therefore there was great mourning in Israel, in every place where they were; so that the princes and elders mourned, the virgins and young men were made feeble, and the beauty of women was changed. Every bridegroom took up lamentation, and she that sat in the marriage chamber was in heaviness. The land also was moved for the inhabitants thereof, and all the house of Jacob was covered with confusion (1 Mac 1:25-28).

These offerings were so important to the priests that they refused to delay them even when the city of Jerusalem was attacked by Pompey in 63 B.C., a century after Antiochus's desecration of the Temple. During this siege the Romans used several kinds of projectile equipment on the city. They had the ballista which could throw stones weighing up to 660 pounds a distance of 650 yards. However, it was the onager which hurled a constant barrage of smaller stones into the city. In spite of the rain of these lethal missiles, the sacrifices continued in the Temple's open courtyard as stones fell about the ministering priests.[6] The offerings were more important than life itself. The priests would not neglect them even to find shelter from the incessant pelting of the stones.

Titus strangled Jerusalem again in A.D. 70. Famine raged. Josephus says,

> And famine increased its dimensions, and devoured the people by whole houses and families; the roofs were full of women and children that were dying of starvation, and the lanes of the city were full of dead bodies of the aged; the children also and the young men wandered about the market place like shadows, all wasted away with famine, and fell down dead, wherever death seized them.[7]

And yet, the priests continued the sacrifices and offerings in the Temple until the last of the animals, grain, and wine were consumed, not by the starving populace, but in the Temple ritual. Fulfilling the ritual requirements of the God of Israel was more important than satisfying the hunger of the people.

One more time this sorrow will overtake the priests. During the Tribulation period the Temple will be rebuilt under the auspices of the Antichrist. Then, midway into the Tribulation period, the Antichrist will break the covenant which he will have made with the Jews. It will be under his patronage that the sacrifices will resume after many centuries. However, the oblations will again cease (Dan 9:27). The consternation of the priests will be great, as great in that day as it was in the days of Joel.

In addition to the locust plague which caused the drunkards, the priests, and the farmers great anguish, Joel also indicated that a severe drought may have ravaged the land at the same time the locusts passed over it. He said,

> O LORD, to thee do I cry; for the fire hath devoured the pastures of the wilderness, and the flame hath burned all the trees of the field. Yea, the beasts of the field pant unto

thee: for the water brooks are dried up, and fire hath devoured the pastures of the wilderness (1:19-20).

These two calamities—the locust plague and drought—had combined to lay upon Judah the worst disaster in memory. And apparently nothing ever again approached the intensity of the insect holocaust and drought which came upon Judah during the ninth century B.C. in the days of Joel the prophet. This is why he began his prophecy by saying,

> Hear this, ye old men, and give ear, all ye inhabitants of the land. Hath this been in your days, or in the days of your fathers? Tell ye your children of it, and let your children tell their children, and their children another generation. That which the palmer-worm hath left hath the locust eaten; and that which the locust hath left hath the canker-worm eaten; and that which the canker-worm hath left hath the caterpillar eaten (1:2-4).

Later, Joel observed, "There hath not been ever the like, neither shall be any more after them, even to the years of many generations" (2:2).

Jesus indicated that when the Day of the Lord actually does come, Israel will know again similar days of anguish during the Great Tribulation period (Mt 24:21).

Joel described the results of this unprecedented drought and insect invasion, saying,

> Is not the food cut off before your eyes, yea, joy and gladness from the house of our God? The seeds rot under their clods; the garners are laid desolate, the barns are broken down; for the grain is withered. How do the beasts groan! The herds of cattle are perplexed, because they have no pasture; yea, the flocks of sheep are made desolate (1:16-18).

The cattle may have been perplexed, but the people did not need to be! The Lord had raised up a prophet, along with the drought and plague, who would interpret to them the meaning of this calamity. The plague came to Judah, but at the same time, "The word of the LORD . . . came to Joel the son of Pethuel" (1:1).

God always has a man to interpret the crisis. The prophets of Israel were all such men. Most of them were called upon the stage of history to proclaim the word of the Lord in the midst of crisis and to declare to the people that their suffering was a result of sin. The prophets usually pointed the way out of the crisis also. In addition, they predicted a better day for Israel in the future.

Here was the ministry of the Hebrew prophet. It was first of all a ministry to the people of his day in which he injected the word of the Lord into the current scene. He proclaimed the will of God to the people during a critical juncture of their history, whatever the crisis might be—the Assyrian crisis in the days of Isaiah, the Babylonian crisis during the days of Jeremiah, or the locust crisis during the days of Joel. These emergencies became the occasion for a fresh hearing of the word of the Lord from the prophet as he interpreted earthly events in spiritual terms, calling upon the people to repent.

But the ministry of the prophet was also predictive. He injected hope into the current crisis by predicting a glorious day for Israel in the distant future. Predictions of a golden age were made by Israel's later prophets in association with the Messianic hope. For a great Deliverer will arise in the house of David to emancipate God's covenant people who are oppressed.

Each of the prophets of Israel followed this pattern. They spoke the word of the Lord to their contemporaries. They also introduced the element of prediction. This carried the prophet's message into the future and also tended to universalize it.

Joel was no exception. He preached to the people of Judah in the ninth century B.C. But he also speaks to the people of the twentieth century A.D., for much of what Joel said is yet to come to pass.

This was the calling of Joel during the plague years.

Daniel Defoe was a child when the bubonic plague—the black death—devastated England during the reign of Charles II. It began in the spring of 1665. At its height there were an estimated 7,000 deaths per week in London alone. By December, London, which was Europe's largest city with a population of over half a million, was nearly deserted. More than 100,000 Londoners had perished in the great plague.

A few years later Daniel Defoe wrote *A Journal of the Plague Year.* Though it was a clever hoax, the journal contained precise descriptions of the frightened populace who fled the city to live in caves and makeshift huts in the countryside. The story is vivid, as Defoe mentions names, dates, and exact details. He tells of Dr. Heath who remained behind to care for the sick and to study the pestilence. Sexton John Haywood walked by the death cart, ringing a bell, to warn any who might be in the street that an infected corpse is coming by.

Defoe lived and wrote in the didactic age of English literature. His novels are noted for their moralizing. However, his general moralizations are vague and their impact muted compared to the prophet Joel who also wrote about a crisis, the locust plague. The prophet's theme is concise and clear. This calamity had spiritual overtones, he affirmed. This was the Day of the Lord upon Israel—unless!

The prophet hinted at the meaning of the plague in 1:15 when he said, "Alas for the day! For the day of the LORD is at hand, and as destruction from the Almighty shall it come." Then he surrounded his dramatic picture of the locust invasion with the spiritual lessons which he had been raised up to declare.

Joel used four figures to depict the terrible incursion of locusts. First, they were like a storm (2:2). Their coming brought a "day of darkness and gloominess, a day of clouds and thick darkness" (2:2). The prophet Zephaniah used these same figures as he also spoke of the coming Day of the Lord (Zep 1:15). But, for Joel, these four synonyms—darkness, gloominess, clouds, and thick darkness—served to emphasize the intense and impenetrable darkness of the locust swarm. The writer of Deuteronomy used three of these words to describe the darkness which enveloped Mount Sinai (Deu 4:11). The fourth word is used to describe the plague of darkness in Egypt (Ex 10:22).

So intense were these figures that some expositors believe that Joel was going beyond current events and was actually depicting an apocalyptic event. But apparently Joel did not exaggerate the darkness which a cloud of locusts can inflict upon a land as they literally blot out the sun and turn the atmosphere into the darkness of a terrible storm. The *National Geographic* Magazine reported on the great locust plague of 1915 which enveloped all of Palestine. In this article the writer concentrated upon the insects' conquest of Jerusalem.

> In Jerusalem the first were seen on Monday of the first day of March at noon. Attention was drawn to them by the sudden darkening of the bright sunshine, and then by the veritable shower of their excretions, which fell thick and fast. . . . At times their elevation was in the hundreds of feet; at other times they came down quite low, detached members alighting. The clouds of them would be so dense as to appear quite black.[8]

Second, Joel said that the coming of the locusts was like fire (2:3). "A fire devoureth before them; and behind them a flame burneth." The Romans called them "the burners of the land," which is the literal meaning of the word "locust." Before the locusts lay a land as the Garden of Eden, the prophet said. Nothing escaped. Everything was combustible in the face of their ravaging.

A locust can eat the equivalent of its own body weight in a

single day. A swarm weighing twenty thousand tons, as many
of them do, will consume forty million pounds of green vege-
tation each day. After they have passed over a garden like
Eden, there is only a desolate wilderness left. The Arabs call
the locust *Jarad*. This name comes from a word which means
"to scrape clean." Like strip miners, they can wipe a landscape clear. When they pass over a garden like Eden it dis-
appears as if by magic.

The prophet Ezekiel used this same idea, but inverted. Re-
versing Joel's imagery, Ezekiel viewed Israel after the Day
of the Lord will be over. He declared that after the apocalyptic Day of the Lord upon the nations, when God will have
regathered Israel and given the people a new heart, "They
shall say, This land that was desolate is become like the garden of Eden" (Eze 36:35).

Joel used a third figure: "The appearance of them is as
the appearance of horses; and as horsemen, so do they run"
(2:4). Many have observed that the head of the locust is
shaped like that of a horse. This is a metaphor which is still
familiar to the Arabs. They say that in the locust, small as it
is, there is the nature of ten of the larger animals. For the
locust has the face of a horse, the eyes of an elephant, the neck
of a bull, the horns of a deer, the chest of a lion, the belly of a
scorpion, the wings of an eagle, the thighs of a camel, the
feet of an ostrich, and the tail of a serpent.

Joel's final figure is that of an invading army (2:6-11). This
is his best image, but it has caused the most difficulty. Some
students of his book have taken these words as apocalyptic
and assume that Joel was using the figure of the locusts to
talk about a literal army which invades Judah.

Joel's vivid portrayal and startling imagery of locusts as an
invading army have given rise to several different interpretations of this passage. Is this invasion an actual plague, and
does Joel's use of heightened imagery depict only an historical
event? Or, are Joel's figures apocalyptic also? Perhaps they

are even allegorical, as the rabbis have said. These are the three ways in which Joel's description of the locust plague, especially in chapter 2, has been taken.

Among those interpreters of the book of Joel who hold the allegorical view of the locust plague were the Jewish commentators, the Targums, and some of the patristic commentators. A few modern scholars have also taken this position; Professor E. B. Pusey is among them. Most of the allegorical interpreters maintain that the locusts are symbols for foreign armies which successively ravaged Judah. Since two passages in Joel (1:4; 2:25) use four different words for locusts, it has been most alluring to see in these four words an allegorical reference to Judah's four great enemies—Babylon, Persia, Greece, and Rome. Jerome says that the rabbis believed that the palmerworm represented all of Israel's former enemies, including the Babylonians, down to the time of the exile. Commenting on Joel 1:4, Jerome wrote,

> Moreover they interpret the locust as the Medes and Persians, who, after the empire of the Chaldeans having been destroyed, held the Jews captive. They interpret the cankerworm as the Macedonians and all the successors of Alexander, especially King Antiochus, with the surname Epiphanes, who like the canker-worm settled on Judea and devoured all the remains of the former kings, under whom are narrated the wars of the Maccabees. The caterpillar they relate to the empire of the Romans, who fourth and last, so far crushed the Jews, that they drove them from their land.[9]

This interpretation was held by some of the rabbis even during the Middle Ages. Rabbi Lehrman says that this view "is favored by Jepheth b. Ali, the leading Karaite commentator on the Bible, whose excellent commentary is coloured by the belief that the four species of locusts mentioned in the Book symbolize the four invasions Judea would undergo at the hands of her enemies."[10]

The rabbis called Babylon, Persia, Greece, and Rome "The Four Kingdoms." The four kingdoms were future enemies of Judah from the standpoint of Joel's day, in the ninth century B.C. But from our vantage point, they have all long since passed off the stage of history. Therefore the *allegorical* interpretation looks back to the invading armies of nations now long dead. But, in contrast to this, the *apocalyptic* interpretation sees in the locust metaphors a picture of an eschatological invasion of Judah that is still future. The locusts are like the nations which will come upon the land as a part of the affliction of the Day of the Lord.

Apocalyptic literature takes its name from a Greek word, *apokalypsis,* which means "unveiling" or "revelation." The apocalyptic material in the Old Testament reveals the events of the future, especially those events which surround the Day of the Lord and the establishment of the Kingdom—to use New Testament concepts, those events which involve the great Tribulation period, the second coming of Christ, and the Millennium. Apocalyptic literature contains predictive prophecy. But it does more. It uses symbols to outline the course of history and to describe the climactic events of the last days. It is for this reason that the apocalyptic issue is raised in the interpretation of Joel 2:1-11. Are the locusts symbols of an invading army which will come upon Israel in the last days? While chapter 3 indicates that armies will invade Israel in the last days, it does so in the verbal terminology of predictive prophecy, but not in apocalyptic, for Joel used no symbols there. The apocalyptic issue has to do with 2:1-11 only. Are the locusts which appear there literal or apocalyptic figures?

In examining the apocalyptic interpretation, the question is not, Does the book of Joel contain prophecy? It does. Chapter 3 is predictive prophecy which describes a future invasion of Israel in the last days.

Rather, the question now is, Is chapter 2 apocalyptic prophecy, and does it refer to a future invading army under the symbol of locusts? Or does chapter 2 merely continue the description of the historic plague? The apocalyptic interpretation assumes that Joel quit depicting the locust plague of his day in chapter 1, and in 2:1-11 he was picturing the destruction which will be caused by an invading army during the last days.

In 2:1-11 the dramatic portrayal of the encroaching locusts does seem to exceed the bounds of reality. He called the locusts "mighty men" and "men of war." He called them "his army," that is, the Lord's army. He described them marching in unbroken ranks. No weapon which Judah could employ would avail against them. Joel even used apocalyptic symbols when he said, "The earth quaketh before them; the heavens tremble; the sun and the moon are darkened, and the stars withdraw their shining" (2:10).

However, an army is an appropriate metaphor for the locusts. It is generally understood that such a description is fitting for an actual invasion of these insects. The Arabs call the locusts another name, *Jaish Allah,* which means "God's army." They even claim that they can find the word *askar,* which means "soldier," written in Arabic on the locust's wings. During the plague of 1915 an old Arab appeared to a group of locust fighters on Mount Scopus and derided them for their efforts.

> One evening . . . while fighting the locusts on Scopus, the mountain adjoining Olivet to the north . . . an aged *fellah* walked up, and notwithstanding the wholesale capture befalling the locusts, broke out with: "All this is of no use; go home and rest; you can do nothing. They are Allah's Army and once they fly they will destroy everything."[11]

There are other things that might indicate that chapter 2 is apocalyptic. For example, Joel called the locusts "the northern army" (2:20). Ordinarily locusts have not invaded Israel from the north, but armies have. However, our observer of the 1915 plague throws some light upon this problem:

> These flying clouds of locusts, in Jerusalem at least, invariably came from the northeast going toward the southwest. . . . Students of Joel . . . find a difficulty in the verse, "And the northerner will I remove far from you," since locusts were reported to invade Palestine from the south; the present experience not only removes this difficulty but establishes the accuracy of Joel's account.[12]

Professor Hubbard sums up these two interpretations by saying,

> For want of stronger evidence to sustain the allegorical and apocalyptic viewpoints, it seems safe to hold that the locusts of Joel are literal insects which, on this particular occasion, came in successive waves over a period of more than a year ("I will restore to you the years"—2:25) and which may have entered Palestine from the North (2:20) rather than from the South, their more usual point of entry. The prophet sees the calamitous havoc which they work as an harbinger of the day of the LORD which is to bring destruction from the Almighty.[13]

Hence, 2:1-11 is to be taken as *actual,* rather than as allegorical or apocalyptic. Joel merely continued his description of the locust plague in chapter 2. This passage does have significance for predictive prophecy, however, but that significance does not lie in the locust being a symbol of an invading army. Rather, the importance of Joel's use of the locust plague is that this plague, while not a symbol, does foreshadow the devastation of the eschatological Day of the Lord. The locusts do not represent the destruction caused by an invading army in the last days so much as they are a foretaste of what will come—though greatly intensified—in the Day of the Lord.

When Joel saw Judah inundated by the plague of locusts in his day, he cried,

> Alas for the day! For the day of the LORD is at hand, and as destruction from the Almighty shall it come. Blow ye the trumpet in Zion, and sound an alarm in my holy mountain; let all the inhabitants of the land tremble: for the day of the LORD cometh, for it is nigh at hand; a day of darkness and gloominess, a day of clouds and thick darkness, as the dawn spread upon the mountains; a great people and a strong; there hath not been ever the like, neither shall be any more after them, even to the years of many generations. . . . For the day of the LORD is great and very terrible; and who can abide it? (Joel 1:15; 2:1-11).

Whether the locust plague occurred in the ninth century B.C. or in 1845 or in 1915, it is a contemporary event with spiritual overtones. Each crisis could be the occasion for the Day of the Lord. So far, the day has not come. In the day of the prophet Joel it was averted by a change of mind on the part of the people. Yet, though none of these past events was the actual Day of the Lord, each contained a foretaste of that day. None was *the* Day of the Lord, but all were *a* day of the Lord in which the Lord demonstrated His potential for judgment.

Therefore each generation should see in the crisis of its own day—whether that crisis be a natural devastation, social or economic disaster, or the destruction caused by a great war—a precursor of final judgment. Each of these is *a* day of the Lord. One of them will issue in *the* Day of the Lord when the patience of God will be long-suffering no more.

3

THE AVERTING OF THE DAY OF THE LORD

Joel 1:13-14; 2:12-17

Dov Baer was a famous Hasidic rabbi in Eastern Europe during the eighteenth century. He said of repentance,

> One man was influenced by the call of conscience to repent. Another went to a tavern to drown his conscience in strong drink. The first is like a horse which, guided by the reins, turns into the right road; the second is like a horse, which, feeling the pull of the rein, steps from the road into a ditch.

Israel has acted like both of these horses.

So have others.

Joel, using different metaphors than those of the rabbi, presented the right road and the ditch in terms of the alternatives of blessing and judgment, with repentance as the catalyst.

John the Baptist appeared in the Jordan Valley declaring that the Kingdom was at hand, calling upon the people to repent. He said,

> And even now the axe lieth at the root of the trees: every tree therefore that bringeth not forth good fruit is hewn down, and cast into the fire. I indeed baptize you in water unto repentance: but he that cometh after me is mightier

40

than I, whose shoes I am not worthy to bear: he shall baptize you in the Holy Spirit and in fire: whose fan is in his hand, and he will thoroughly cleanse his threshing-floor; and he will gather his wheat into the garner, but the chaff he will burn up with unquenchable fire (Mt 3:10-12).

John's words about the coming of the Kingdom are clear: the Kingdom is at hand because the King is at hand.

But what does it mean to be baptized "in the Holy Spirit and in fire"? Are these alternatives? Or do "Spirit" and "fire" refer to the same experience?

The single preposition which John used might indicate that the baptism "in the Holy Spirit and in fire" is not one of alternatives, but refers to one and the same experience. If this is so, then "fire" stands for some phase of the Spirit's work. Perhaps it is a symbol for cleansing or for energizing or some other work of the Spirit which one must arbitrarily invest in the symbol of fire. If this is correct, then John's words about the Spirit and fire mean that Jesus would baptize the believer in the Spirit, resulting in cleansing or energizing or in whatever else fire is supposed to symbolize.

But we must remember that John the Baptist was preaching to a single class of people, the Jews. He was declaring to them the possibility of the Messianic Kingdom, that golden age toward which all the prophets looked. This one group, the Jews, is destined to receive a baptism. However, this baptism is composed of two alternatives, observes Dr. Broadus.[1] Which of these alternatives prevails is contingent upon whether the Jews repent at the preaching of the Gospel. They will be baptized in the Spirit *if* they repent and accept Jesus as their Messiah and Saviour, or they will be baptized in fire *if* they do not. Therefore "fire" must stand for an alternative to "Spirit." That alternative is judgment. Fire is a symbol for this judgment, which will come if the Spirit does not come.

However, the most convincing indication that John's figure of "fire" stands for an alternative of judgment rather than for a result of being baptized with the Spirit is found in the context. Here John unquestionably used the term "fire" in the sense of judgment. In Matthew 3:10 John said, "And even now the axe lieth at the root of the trees: every tree therefore that bringeth not forth good fruit is hewn down, and cast into the *fire.*" Again, in 3:12, which follows John's statement about the "Holy Spirit and fire," he said, "Whose fan is in his hand, and he will thoroughly cleanse his threshing-floor; and he will gather his wheat into the garner, but the chaff he will burn up with unquenchable *fire.*" Twice John clearly used the word "fire" to stand for judgment in two of these three verses. It is a fair assumption then that the third use of "fire," in verse 11, also stands for judgment.

John's message to the Jews was this: Repent and be immersed in the Spirit. If you do not repent, then you will be immersed in fire (judgment). John was emphasizing the two alternatives—the Spirit or fire, blessing or judgment—which continually confront the nation Israel.

But where did John the Baptist get this idea? Was it original with him? Or do its antecedents trail back into the Old Testament?

This theme extends backward for 800 years into the theology of the book of Joel. How did the prophet Joel develop these alternatives? His overview of the Day of the Lord has several ingredients. First, on the basis of the locust plague, it was revealed to him that this crisis could become *the* Day of the Lord. However, if the current critical situation did not develop into *the* Day of the Lord, then it still was a type of that day. Therefore, every critical juncture which confronts the people during the course of their history is *a* contemporary day of the Lord. It is also a precursor of *the* Day of the Lord. Hence, the locust plague, which occurred in Joel's time, could have developed into *the* Day of the Lord. But it did not. Nevertheless, it remains a harbinger of that day.

Why did not the locust plague develop into *the* day? Because the Day of the Lord can also be averted by repentance which can change the threat of judgment into the promise of blessing. Israel repented and therefore the threat of the day subsided. In addition, when repentance thorough enough to postpone the Day of the Lord occurred, it was also dynamic enough to bring about a time of blessing from the Lord. Repentance can move the issue from the negative of judgment to the positive of blessing. It is that dynamic. It occupies a place of great importance in God's dealing with man, for genuine repentance is sufficient to alter the plan of God, at least for the moment. Consequently, when the people of Judah repented, they were promised an alternative—the day of the Spirit (blessing) in the place of the Day of the Lord (judgment). This is the second feature of the Day of the Lord brought out in the theology of Joel.

Third, repentance cannot delay the Day of the Lord indefinitely. It was revealed to Joel that the day will come eventually. When it does, it is to be a day of destruction. Amos clearly saw this. Apparently the people of Amos's day were interpreting the Day of the Lord exclusively as one of blessing. But the prophet said,

> Woe unto you that desire the day of the LORD! Wherefore would ye have the day of the LORD? It is darkness, and not light. As if a man did flee from a lion, and a bear met him; or went into the house and leaned his hand on the wall, and a serpent bit him. Shall not the day of the LORD be darkness, and not light? Even very dark, and no brightness in it? (Amos 5:18-20).

But even then, Joel added, "Whosoever shall call on the name of the Lord shall be delivered" (2:32).

Finally, the great upheaval of the Day of the Lord is to be followed by the golden age of the Messiah's reign.

This is the meaning of the day as it was revealed to Joel.

Now, what did this mean for the nation Israel? It meant

that the two alternatives—Spirit or fire, blessing or judgment—were faced by the people of Joel's day just as they were faced by the Jews in the day of John the Baptist.

In Joel's day the people repented when threatened by the Day of the Lord. Their repentance was not only thorough enough to avert judgment, but it was also dynamic enough to produce God's positive blessings. When Judah repented, promised blessings replaced promised judgment. The locust plague was lifted, and the land was restored to productivity.

An additional part of the blessing was that Judah was also promised the Spirit. This was to be a future benefit which would come to the people. This promise was *partially* fulfilled in the first century A.D. when many individual Jews, through repentance and faith, received Jesus as Messiah and Saviour. They also received the Spirit, which was poured out at Pentecost. However, Joel's prediction will not be *completely* fulfilled until the Messianic era is ushered in at the second coming of Christ. This is why the apocalyptic symbols accompany the promise of the Spirit in Joel (cf. Joel 2:30-31; Ac 2:19-20). The prophet Ezekiel spoke of that day like this:

> And ye shall know that I am the LORD, when I have opened your graves, and caused you to come up out of your graves, O my people. And I will put my Spirit in you, and ye shall live, and I will place you in your own land: and ye shall know that I, the LORD, have spoken it and performed it, saith the LORD (Eze 37:13-14).

Individual Jews, members of the Body of Christ, were given the Spirit at Pentecost. But they are hardly representative of the whole nation Israel. Then what about Israel nationally?

When Simon Peter said that the Pentecostal advent of the Holy Spirit *fulfilled* Joel's prophecy, did he mean that it *exhausted* Joel's prophecy? After all, the apocalyptic signs (Joel 2:30-31; Ac 2:19-20) were not fulfilled in the day of Pentecost. Since they are an inseparable part of the Spirit's promise, their absence at historical Pentecost must be explained by the fact that much of Old Testament predictive prophecy is capable of a dual fulfillment. A *partial* fulfillment may occur at any given time in history, while an *ultimate* fulfillment will come later. Joel's prediction about the coming of the Spirit was fulfilled in the individual believer at Pentecost. Yet, it is to have a later and a national fulfillment in Israel. Joel's prediction about the coming of the Spirit was *partially* fulfilled at Pentecost when individual Jews received the Spirit. But it will also have an *ultimate* fulfillment in the nation when Israel receives the Spirit at the second coming of Christ. Zechariah said,

> And I will pour upon the house of David, and upon the inhabitants of Jerusalem, the spirit of grace and of supplication; and they shall look unto me whom they have pierced; and they shall mourn for him, as one mourneth for his only son, and shall be in bitterness for him, as one that is in bitterness for his first-born (Zec 12:10).

At the cross, when Israel's Messiah was cut off and the Kingdom postponed, the Jews entered into an era of judicial blindness (Ro 11:25). God ceased to deal with His covenant people. During the great parenthesis—the age of the Church—God is calling out a new people for His name (Ac 15:14). They too are receiving the Spirit, for every born-again believer is indwelt by the Holy Spirit. When the Body of Christ, the Church, is completed, these believers will be caught out of the world to meet the Lord Jesus in the air. This will be the rapture (1 Th 4:16-17). Then God will turn once more to deal with Israel nationally.

In the Great Tribulation period (Rev 11-18) Israel will again face the impending Day of the Lord. Even then, Joel's theme is to be played out still another time, for some Jews will repent. They will receive the Spirit. Others will not repent. At the close of the Tribulation period the judgment of the Day of the Lord will finally come upon Israel nationally, for in that day the Jews will have faced again the two alternatives. The faithful remnant who repent will go into the Messianic Kingdom, having been redeemed and having received the Spirit. They are the recipients of the blessing phase of the Day of the Lord. But during the Great Tribulation many Jews will accept the mark of the beast (Rev 13:1-17). This will indicate that they have yielded to the Antichrist as god (1 Jn 2:22; 4:3). On these representatives of apostate Israel, the judgment phase of the Day of the Lord will finally come.

We conclude, therefore, that while we are indebted to other Old Testament prophets as well as to the New Testament for further light on the meaning of the Day of the Lord, it is the prophet Joel who gives us the basic pattern of the day. It was he who saw the antithesis between the outpoured Spirit (blessing) and the outpoured wrath (judgment), with repentance as the spiritual catalyst determining which alternative is to prevail.

The prophet Joel's thesis was that repentance would bring the day of the Spirit, while nonrepentance would bring the Day of the Lord. John, the forerunner of the Messiah, picked up this theme and used it to declare to his contemporaries in Israel that they were facing the same options which the people of Joel's days had faced. To the Jews of his day, John the Baptist proclaimed, "I indeed baptize you in water unto repentance: but he that cometh after me is mightier than I, whose shoes I am not worthy to bear: he shall baptize you in the Holy Spirit and in fire" (Mt 3:11). This idea is also repeated in the sermon which Simon Peter preached on the day of Pentecost, "Repent ye . . . and ye shall receive the gift of the Holy Spirit" (Ac 2:38). Individual Jews repented and received Jesus as the Messiah. They also received the Spirit on the day of Pentecost. Others of the Jews did not repent. They received fire—*a* day of the Lord upon Israel—when the second Temple fell, the city was destroyed by the Romans, and the people of Israel were driven into their second exile (Mt 23:38).

This same scenario is to be repeated again at the end of the age, as once more the Jews will be confronted with the two alternatives: Spirit or fire, blessings or judgment. Through the ministry of the 144,000, Israel will hear the word: "Repent and receive the Spirit! If you do not repent, you will receive the Day of the Lord!" A faithful remnant in Israel will repent and the Spirit will be poured out upon them according to the prophet Ezekiel, who said,

> And they shall know that I am the Lord their God, in that I caused them to go into captivity among the nations, and have gathered them unto their own land; and I will leave none of them any more there; neither will I hide my face any more from them: for I have poured out my Spirit upon the house of Israel, saith the Lord God (Eze 39:28-29).

Other Jews will find no repentance. Consequently they will know the judgment of the Day of the Lord, along with the Gentile nations. Three events—the Great Tribulation, the Battle of Armageddon, and the second coming of Christ—constitute the Day of the Lord upon the Gentile nations and upon unrepentant Israel.

In the prophet's development of this antithesis between the outpoured Spirit and the outpoured wrath, Joel presented an outline of God's prophetic program for Israel and for the nations during the last days. He revealed that unrepentant Israel and the nations will go down in defeat and be destroyed, while those in Israel who repent at the coming of the Messiah will receive the Spirit and enter into the golden age.

These truths, which are made explicit in the New Testament, are already present in the Old Testament, especially in the book of Joel. They all started when Joel saw more than a local disaster in an avalanche of locusts. Through this crisis the Lord revealed to him the great prophetic theme which will determine the destiny of the covenant people Israel as well as the Gentile nations.

John the Baptist preached, Repent, for the Kingdom is at hand (Mk 1:15).

Joel the prophet preached, Repent, for the Day of the Lord is at hand (Joel 1:15).

After these men preached, the events about which they were preaching were postponed. The Kingdom of God was delayed in John's day because Israel did not repent. The Day of the Lord was delayed in Joel's day because Israel did repent.

Here is the power of repentance.

Rabbi Nachman says, "Repentance is a cure for the ills of humanity." Joel's call to repentance cured the ills of his day and turned aside the climactic judgment of the Day of the Lord. He issued this call to repentance twice during the great locust plague.

His first call to repentance is found in 1:13-14. Joel said,

> Gird yourselves with a sackcloth, and lament, ye priests; wail, ye ministers of the altar; come, lie all night in sackcloth, ye ministers of my God: for the meal-offering and the drink-offering are withholden from the house of your God. Sanctify a fast, call a solemn assembly, gather the old men and all the inhabitants of the land unto the house of the LORD your God, and cry unto the LORD.

In this first call to repentance there is a contrast between Joel's use of "my God" and "your God." This contrast is between the prophet's God and the priest's God. God is the same, yet their conception of Him differed.

The God of the priests was believed to be a God who was primarily concerned with the drink offerings and the meal offerings. It was thought that he was offended when these ceased, as they did during the plague and drought.

In contrast, the God of the prophet was offended by the attitude of the priests and the people. Their problem was not empty altars, but empty hearts. Though the empty altars may have called for restoration of the sacrifices, it was their sin which was the real problem. Repentance, not sacrifice, was needed. The same idea is found in Hosea. He said, "For I desire goodness, and not sacrifice; and knowledge of God more than burnt-offerings" (Ho 6:6). Jesus repeated this indictment to the Jews of His day (Mt 9:13; 12:7).

Joel's initial call to repentance has a dual emphasis.

First, it was to begin with the religious leaders rather than with the people. It was to affect the people, but it had to start at the top and filter downward.

One of the most famous engravings of England's evangelical revival in the eighteenth century pictures John Wesley standing upon a slab of stone above his father's grave, preaching. A little girl once pondered this picture, then said, "What's he doing there?" Wesley, preaching on the top of his father's grave, is a key to the orientation of the evangelical revival in the mid-1700s. He was there because the door of the established church in Epworth, as well as all over England, was closed to him. Called the Great Awakening, it did not spread from priest to people. Rather, it remained a people's movement. Unlike Wesley, many of the priests of the Establishment were not affected by it. Most were even hostile toward it, crying in histrionic alarm, "Enthusiasm! Enthusiasm!"

Apparently the reverse was true in Joel's day. The awakening spread from the priests to the people. This was the route which the prophet intended it to take, for he began by calling the religious leaders to repentance.

Joel's call had another emphasis also. It was active rather than academic. He emphasized what the priests were to do rather than what they were to say. In fact, the word "repentance" was not even used with reference to the priests or the people. In his second call Joel did talk about God repent-

ing. But he never used this word in his instructions to priests
or people. Joel did not talk theology, but action. In 1:13-14
he placed the emphasis upon the outward indications of repentance rather than on the inward principle. In his second
call he dealt with the inward side of repentance, but in the
first call it was all pragmatic. Action was needed. Later a theology could be formulated, but first they had to do something
quickly, for the emergency of the plague and the drought was
upon them. It was an immediate disaster. After a while they
could formulate a doctrine of repentance and thus clarify
their beliefs. But first, the activity of repentance had to precede the academics of repentance. Subsequently, the theology
professors could reflect on what had happened. But right
then it had to happen. In the years that lay ahead, a systematic
theology of the locust plague could be produced. But first the
religious leaders had to act rather than speculate.

The evangelical revival was inductive. It spread from the
people up to the priests, that is, to those priests who were affected. And it had great and lasting effects upon the Church
of Jesus Christ, both in Europe and in America. But nothing
has ever affected the spiritual life of the Church like the
Reformation. And it was a spiritual awakening which spread
from the religious leaders to the people, just as the revival of
Joel's day did. Either direction will get results. But a deduc-
tive route—from the priests to the people—seems to have the
potential for a more lasting impact. A lay awakening which
induces the clergy to repent can be greatly used of the Spirit
of God. However, God's order seems to be the reverse: an
awakening which spreads from the religious leaders to the
people. This was the nature of the awakening of Joel's day,
for it is evident in the prophet's instructions to the priests and
the ministers.

The order of repentance is very clear in these verses. At
the top are the priests and the ministers. "Gird yourselves
with sackcloth, and lament, ye priests; wail, ye ministers of

the altar." Next the old men are to be involved. "Gather the old men." Then, finally, all the inhabitants of the land were to come to the house of God. "Gather . . . all the inhabitants of the land."

In the Lord's house—the Temple—they were to cry out to Him.

The Midrash says, "The solemn gathering is the most important part of a fast."[2] The rabbis recognized that a spiritual experience was best maintained and perpetuated in a corporate way. Joel saw this also. Notice that the spiritual awakening was to center in the house of God and not among isolated individuals or groups. The sanctuary was its focal point. Periodically revivals will erupt outside the Church, among individual believers, in small lay-oriented groups, meeting on what may be called secular ground. But again, the most responsible of spiritual awakenings center within the structure of the Church. A revival within the historic Church is given responsible guidelines. Occasionally a revival may create a new church, as it did during the Reformation and the evangelical revival. But even these become the frame of reference to contain the awakening, give it responsible direction, perpetuate its truths, and retain its effects. We are the beneficiaries of Reformation truths today because of this. Four hundred years after the Reformation we are guided by *sola Scriptura*, the Bible only. We believe the Bible to be the objective and infallible rule of faith and practice, because this heritage of the revival of the sixteenth century was passed down to us through the structure of the Church. We also believe that God's saving activity is outside of us in the person of Jesus Christ who is the sole ground of salvation, *sola gratia*. This, too, is a Reformation heritage passed down to all evangelical churches through a channel which involves a historic church structure. However, an awakening which does not relate itself to an established church cuts itself off from that which can conserve its impetus and prevent this dynamic from dissipating. Outside the Church it will finally burn itself out, leaving nothing but the memory of religious excitement.

That was why Joel wanted the revival to occur in the house of God. There its results would be most pointedly felt and retained and passed on to future generations in the most responsible of ways.

Joel's second call to repentance (2:12-17) contains several features. The first and most obvious lesson is that the grace of God is patient with our delay.

Past sin brought about the punishment which Judah was then experiencing through the locust plague. But God "is longsuffering . . . not wishing that any should perish, but that all should come to repentance" (2 Pe 3:9). He had already issued, through His servant, the prophet Joel, a first call to repentance. Apparently this first call was ineffective, probably because the punishment was not yet severe enough to produce a contrite attitude.

The plague intensified. This accounts for the heightened imagery of 2:1-11. Soon the people were ready.

A second call to repent was issued by Joel. This time the word of the Lord was heard and heeded. Often "the goodness of God leadeth . . . to repentance" (Ro 2:4). Sometimes it does not. Then the voice of God had to sound with the stress on judgment. If this also went unheeded, then even harsher accents would be necessary in order that God's voice, calling the people to repentance, might be obeyed.

Though repeated, God's offer of mercy is not limitless. It is placed within the framework of His patience. When His forbearance is exhausted, then the Day of the Lord will come.

An ancient Saxon chronicle tells of a king in whose country a rebellion developed. This king set out with an army to quell the insurrection. Soon things were in his control again, with the rebel army defeated. The king, who had made his headquarters in one of the castles of that distant province, placed a candle in the archway over its entrance. Lighting the candle, he then announced that if all who were in rebellion against him would surrender and take an oath of loyalty while the candle was still burning, they would be spared. Here is clemency, but only for the life of the candle.

This too is the message of Joel. God's call to repentance is heard more than once. But not forever. The Day of the Lord will come, warned Joel.

Joel's words, "Yet even now, saith the Lord, turn ye unto me" (2:12), suggest the potential of true repentance, which can cause God to change His mind. The hour was desperate, but not hopeless. For "yet even now," Joel said, God may repent of the judgment He intends to inflict upon Judah because of her sin.

It has already been pointed out that in Joel's text the word "repent" is used not of man, but of God. The prophet laid the concept of repentance upon man. But Joel reserved the terminology of repentance for God. This suggests that the Hebrew word can be used in a morally neutral sense, meaning simply "to change one's mind." Joel affirmed that God would change His mind about the Day of the Lord—"yet even now" postpone it—if the people would only repent. God changed His mind about the destruction of Nineveh when the people repented at the preaching of Jonah (Jon 3:5-10). He spared the Assyrian capital because the people heeded Jonah's warning. Repentance averts judgment, at least for a while. This also was true in Joel's day, when repentance alone had the potential of forestalling the Day of the Lord.

Joel's second call contains one of the finest definitions of repentance to be found in all the Bible. "Turn ye unto me with all your heart, and with fasting, and with weeping, and with mourning: and rend your heart, and not your garments, and turn unto the LORD your God" (2:12-13).

Joel's figures in verse 12 suggest that repentance involves the entire personality. The "heart" in Hebrew psychology is not the seat of affections, as we sometimes use the word.

Rather, it is an organ of intelligence.[3] Hosea said that "Ephraim is like a silly dove, without understanding (7:11). "Understanding" in Hosea and "heart" in Joel are translated from the same Hebrew word. Joel called for a turning which would include the intelligence. "Fasting" invokes the will. "Weeping" and "mourning" suggest that the emotions are affected.

The mind, the emotions, and the will—the essence of personality—are all a part of repentance, for repentance is a change of mind entailing the emotions, which affects the will, resulting in a redirection of the life. All of this is suggested by the images which Joel used.

This repentance, in order to be meaningful, must be inward. "Rend your heart, and not your garments." Rending of the garments is an outward show of sorrow for what one has *done*. Rending the heart is inward sorrow for what one *is*. Repentance gets one ready, not to *do* something, but to *be* something. *Doing* penance is not as important as *being* penitent. Thus God's judgment is not delayed by what one *does*. Rather, it is what one *becomes* in the act of repentance that forestalls His judgment. After all, God cannot be placated by what we *do*. There is not a spiritual conspiracy in which God's wrath can be bought off by some performance on our part. It is what we become that enables God to postpone judgment and substitute blessings in its place, even as He did in Joel's day.

Repentance enables one to become open and receptive to the movement of God's Spirit. Sin is rebellion; it closes the door. Repentance is submission; it opens the door and presents an unencumbered heart to God in which He can work. When this occurs, judgment is no longer needed, for God's judgments are not arbitrary. His temporal judgments are remedial rather than punitive. Their purpose is to rectify rather than condemn. They are designed to cure rather than to afflict. If repentance leads one to that remedied condition before judgment falls, then temporal judgment is no longer needed. Blessings can now flow in the place of judgment. This was demonstrated in Judah when the blessings of the Lord replaced the Day of the Lord.

Joel presented the Lord's response to true repentance, declaring,"For he is gracious and merciful, slow to anger, and abundant in lovingkindness, and repenteth him of the evil. Who knoweth whether he will not turn and repent, and leave a blessing behind him" (2:13-14) .

The prophet banked on the fact that God is more anxious to bless than to judge. He felt sure that he could predict the response of God.

However, Joel did not anticipate the grace, mercy, and loving-kindness of God in such absolute terms that the people might be tempted to trifle with God. They could not presume that He would change His mind about judgment simply because "he is gracious and merciful, slow to anger, and abundant in lovingkindness." Therefore Joel said, "Who knoweth whether he will not turn and repent, and leave a blessing behind him." He uses "who knoweth" to mean "perhaps," for a more dogmatic assertion could have created false security, causing the people to become reckless. Joel was confident, but not overconfident of God's response. There was just enough of the element of chance in Joel's statement to underscore the need for immediate repentance. Repentance was imperative immediately, for after all, that was the second call. There might not be another. In fact, he said, they could only be reasonably sure that He would change His mind at that late date and turn aside the Day of the Lord.

No one really knows when he has gone too far for repentance to avail. It is possible to go too far. Esau did (Heb 12: 17) .

But, as future events demonstrate, Judah had not gone that

far. Her repentance was effective in countermanding the day.

When individuals repent, it is significant. But when multitudes repent, that is revival.

It was such a corporate spiritual awakening that Joel then urged, "Blow the trumpet in Zion, sanctify a fast, call a solemn assembly: . . . gather the children, and those that suck the breasts: let the bridegroom go forth from his chamber, and the bride out of her closet" (2:15-16).

In 2:1 the trumpet was to be blown to announce the impending day of judgment. But now the trumpet was to be blown to announce the day of revival.

The central Kentucky countryside was hushed in the dead of winter. A snowfall blanketed the rolling bluegrass farms. People were drawn across the winter landscape to a small-town campus. As they approached the auditorium, the crisp and sparkling winter air was intense with stillness, yet charged with excitement. Suddenly the quiet was broken by the thunder of a great organ.

Singing began. "Oh, that will be glory for me!"

The spiritual surge rolled from that assembly out across the campus, so vivid that it swept approaching visitors in its rapture.

Revival had come to Asbury College.

The rolling peal of the organ, whose notes were charged with a spiritual presence, reminded one of Joel's trumpet which had sounded in Zion, calling all the people—old men and children alike—to participate in spiritual awakening.

And thus revival came to Judah 2,800 years ago.

4

THE ALTERNATIVE TO THE DAY OF THE LORD

Joel 2:18-32

THE TALMUD SAYS, "Great is repentance for it reaches the Throne of God."[1]

It did in Joel's day.

This explains the radical change in Judah's fortune, depicted in the remainder of the book. The people repented and the Day of the Lord was averted. In its place blessings, both present and future, were promised. The immediate and temporal blessings are presented in 2:18-27, while the more remote and spiritual blessings are predicted in 2:28-32.

The King James Version records the transition from judgment to blessings in the future tense. However, the American Standard Version rightly changes it to the past tense, saying, "Then was the LORD jealous for his land, and had pity on his people" (2:18). Their repentance had already taken place in response to Joel's preaching. Though it is not stated, it is implied that the people did gather together and that they did follow Joel's instructions. They repented.

Though we do not know how much time elapsed between verses 17 and 18 in chapter 2, evidently the awakening occurred in Judah during this interim.

One summer day a nobleman rode into a little English hamlet. He was hot, tired, and very thirsty. But in this town there was no place to buy liquor. "Why is it that a man cannot find a place to buy a drink in this wretched village?" he asked a peasant. Sensing his nobility, the farmer respectfully replied, "You see, my lord, about a hundred years ago a man named John Wesley came preaching in these parts. There's been no liquor sold here since!"

A century had passed, but the results of the evangelical revival were still being felt. If a spiritual awakening can be judged by its lasting impact, then the revival of Joel's day was one of the greatest in spiritual history. Judah's repentance and subsequent revival brought an awakening whose results we are still witnessing, although twenty-eight centuries have gone by. Every time the Holy Spirit is given, this is a continuing fulfillment of the promise, the ongoing results of the awakening which occurred in Judah in the ninth century B.C.

The first results of Joel's revival were both immediate and temporal. The land was rescued from the invasion of the locusts and from the searing effects of the drought.

This is an emphasis in Joel which has been little noted: the ecology of revival, that is, its healing effects upon the land.

We know that the land was originally cursed by sin. God said to Adam and Eve,

> Cursed is the ground for thy sake; in toil shalt thou eat of it all the days of thy life; thorns also and thistles shalt it bring forth to thee; and thou shalt eat the herb of the field; in the sweat of thy face shalt thou eat bread, till thou return unto the ground (Gen 3:17-19).

The rabbis, commenting on this verse, say,

> Had man not sinned, figtrees, vines, and the pomegranate would have borne fruit on the very day they were planted as it was when the world was created, as stated in Scripture: "Fruit-trees (immediately) bearing fruit after its kind." Had man deserved this boon, it would still be so. Men

would plant trees and they would immediately bear fruit. But when man sinned, the ground was cursed, as it says, "Cursed is the ground for thy sake."[2]

The name Noah means "rest" or "comfort." It was given to Noah for a special reason. Lamech, his father, believed that through his son, Noah, God would somehow relieve the race which struggles against the ground's curse. Lamech "called his name Noah, saying, This same shall comfort us in our work and in the toil of our hands, which cometh because of the ground which the LORD hath cursed" (Gen 5:28-29). Though Noah did nothing to remove the Edenic curse itself, his obedience meant that never again during the course of history would God violently curse the ground with a terminal judgment like the Flood (cf. Gen 8:21).

But what about revival? Can it also influence the physical world? Does spiritual awakening have ecological implications?

Paul indicated that spiritual measures can affect the future of the cursed land. He said,

> For the earnest expectation of the creation waiteth for the revealing of the sons of God. For the creation was subjected to vanity, not of its own will, but by reason of him who subjected it, in hope that the creation itself also shall be delivered from the bondage of corruption into the liberty of the glory of the children of God. For we know that the whole creation groaneth and travaileth in pain together until now (Ro 8:19-22).

Admittedly, the apostle was speaking of the ultimate healing of the earth, which will take place at the second coming of Christ.

The rabbis have noted this. In his Midrash, Rabbi Eliezer says,

> The Holy One, blessed be He, had made me glad and brought me into the garden of Eden, and showed me the place of the abode of the righteous in the garden of Eden, and He showed me the four kingdoms, their rule and their

destruction; and He showed me David, the son of Jesse, and his dominion in the future that is to come."[3]

"Eden" is the place of land blessing. "The four kingdoms" are the conventional enemies of Israel—Babylon, Persia, Greece, and Rome. They are the traditional devastators of the land. "David" is the Messiah, and "the future which is to come" refers to the Messianic age when the land will once again become as Eden (cf. Eze 36:35). In his little vignette, Rabbi Eliezer conveys the principle: the land is blessed in Eden, cursed by sin, and finally blessed again during the Messianic age. However, between these two termini of ultimate land blessing—Eden and the Millennium—partial rejuvenation of the land may be experienced through revival.

The spiritual principle is clear. As we consider the earth, in the beginning cursed by sin, and at the end subject to redemption and blessing, we see that the spirit world can affect the temporal world for good or for evil. At the beginning and at the end of world history spiritual factors determine the earth's destiny. Though both the curse and the blessing are presented in a terminal frame of reference, it is also true that periodic spiritual awakenings can affect the land too. At least the book of Joel strongly hints that this is the case.

Israel's sin brought the locust plague and drought. Her repentance brought healing to the land. Though the final healing will be eschatological, the Bible does seem to indicate that periodic revivals are of ecological value. Apparently they help stabilize the earth, for the land is subject to the laws of the spiritual world. When evil is widespread, the land suffers. But during times of revival, when righteousness prevails, the land is somehow blessed in this association.

We have heard of experiments in which identical plants are grown in differing environments. Some of these plants are nurtured in a hostile atmosphere where anger and curses are showered over them. Others are placed in a loving environment. The latter thrive in the atmosphere of love while the other plants wither away or their growth is stunted. Though the validity of these experiments is yet to be demonstrated, we do know that with respect to the physical body, righteousness tends to health. Sin promotes the breakdown of the physical frame. Though less self-evident, the same thing seems to be true in all the physical realm. Plants, animals, as well as the ground itself, are to prosper during times of revival. Only the intensity, the breadth, and the duration of the revival determine just how far-reaching its ecological effects will be.

This is a major thesis of the book of Joel.

First, as a result of the people repenting, the locusts were removed. Joel called them "the northern army" (2:20). Obviously they invaded Judah from the north. Though this was unusual, it is not without verification. The invasion of locusts in 1915 came from that direction.[4] Joel said,

> I will remove far off from you the northern army, and will drive it into the land barren and desolate, its forepart into the eastern sea, and its hinder part into the western sea; and its stench shall come up, and its ill savor shall come up, because it hath done great things (2:20).

The front ranks of the locust army would be blown into the Dead Sea, "the eastern sea." The remainder of the army would be driven into the Mediterranean, "the western sea." During the fourth century A.D. Jerome observed,

> Even in our times we have seen the land of Judah covered by swarms of locusts, which as soon as the wind arose were precipitated into the first and hindermost seas. And when the shores of both seas were filled with heaps of dead locusts, which the waters had thrown up, their corruption and stench became so noxious that even the atmosphere was corrupted, and both man and beast suffered from subsequent pestilence.[5]

Joel made the same observation about the locusts of his day. "And its stench shall come up, and its ill savor shall come up, because it hath done great things" (2:20*b*).

Second, the land was returned to productivity because the drought was also abated. The rains came. "Be glad then, ye children of Zion, and rejoice in the LORD your God; for he giveth you the former rain in just measure, and he causeth to come down from you the rain, the former rain, and the latter rain, in the first month" (2:23).

Is the earth's atmosphere, as well as the earth itself, affected by revival? Are the effects of revival cosmic as well as ecological?

Obviously God is in sovereign control of the elements. The rain comes at His decree. But is there more? If sin caused the drought, did the awakening itself create conditions conducive to rain and the return of fertility? The prophet Isaiah said that this very thing will happen in the millennial earth when the spiritual atmosphere is made ideal by the Messiah's reign. "For in the wilderness shall waters break out, and streams in the desert. And the glowing sand shall become a pool, and the thirsty ground springs of water: in the habitation of jackals, where they lay, shall be grass with reeds and rushes" (Is 35:6-7). In the millennial earth the standard of righteousness will be realized. This, in turn, will produce blessings in the physical realm. To a lesser degree, spiritual awakenings in history may exercise far more influence upon the elements than we realize. There is just enough hint in the Word to make tenable this cosmic aspect of revival.

Whether by sovereign decree or by the inexorable workings of the laws of revival, during the great awakening of Joel's day there was a dramatic recovery of Judah's agriculture. The prophet said,

> Fear not, O land, be glad and rejoice; for the LORD hath done great things. Be not afraid, ye beasts of the field; for

> the pastures of the wilderness do spring, for the tree beareth
> its fruit, the fig-tree and the vine do yield their strength.
> And the floors shall be full of wheat, and the vats shall
> overflow with new wine and oil. And I will restore to you
> the years that the locust hath eaten (2:21-22, 24-25).

Before the awakening came, Joel instructed the priests to
pray, "Spare thy people, O LORD, and give not thy heritage to
reproach, that the nations should rule over them: wherefore
should they say among the peoples, Where is their God?" (2:
17). Then this reproach was taken away. The revival had returned fertility and stability to the land. The nations witnessed this.

> And ye shall eat in plenty and be satisfied, and shall praise
> the name of the LORD your God, that hath dealt wondrously
> with you; and my people shall never be put to shame. And
> ye shall know that I am in the midst of Israel, and that I am
> the LORD your God, and there is none else; and my people
> shall never be put to shame (2:26-27).

This relationship between the covenant people Israel and
the land was unprecedented. Their unique punishment for
sin was the forfeiture of the land. Their unique blessing
for righteousness was that the land was returned to them and
they were to dwell securely therein.

The Midrash on Psalms says that "three things were given
conditionally (by the Lord): the Land of Israel; the Temple;
and the throne of David."[6] All three will be returned to the
covenant people at the second coming of Christ.

Israel is to find Messianic salvation at the close of the Great
Tribulation. The Jews, purged during the Tribulation, will
accept the Lord Jesus Christ as Messiah and Saviour when He
comes again. However, there will not be a complete fulfillment of Israel's destiny until the spiritual blessings of the last
days include the return of the land. Israel dwelling securely
in the land, made fertile and productive by divine blessing, is

the ultimate sign of God's benediction upon His people. This necessitates the millennial reign of the Lord Jesus Christ. Only then will the Old Testament ideal for Israel be realized and God's care for His covenant people fully vindicated to the nations.

However, a preview of this was experienced in Joel's day as the land was reclaimed through the effects of repentance and revival. Therefore the judgment phase of the Day of the Lord was previewed. But the blessing phase of the day was also disclosed in this little dramatic representation of the Day of the Lord. In Joel's Jerusalem the suffering of the Great Tribulation plagues and the blessings of the Messianic age were both present, for the moment, foreshadowing what is to come in the end time.

The people repented and the fertility of the land was restored to them. This restoration did not last, for their faithfulness to the Lord did not last. They would lose the land many times in the future, both productively, through natural reverses, and actually, through exile. But while it did last, at least for the time, this indicated to the nations that the Lord still cared for His covenant people.

The first result of the people's repentance was temporal and immediate: the land was healed. The second major result was spiritual and future: God would give His Spirit to all the people. Joel said, as he continued to count the consequences of Judah's repentance,

> And it shall come to pass afterward, that I will pour out my Spirit upon all flesh; and your sons and your daughters shall prophesy, your old men shall dream dreams, your young men shall see visions: and also upon the servants and upon the handmaids in those days will I pour out my Spirit (2:28-29).

In addition to experiencing the Spirit, a faithful remnant in Israel will also escape the judgment of the Day of the Lord when it finally comes in the future.

> And I will show wonders in the heavens and in the earth: blood, and fire, and pillars of smoke. The sun shall be turned into darkness, and the moon into blood, before the great and terrible day of the LORD cometh. And it shall come to pass, that whosoever shall call on the name of the LORD shall be delivered (2:30-32).

This section of Joel's prophecy (2:28-32) is chapter 3 in the Hebrew Bible. Its prediction about Judah's spiritual future is twofold: the Spirit will be poured out and those who receive the Spirit—signifying their repentance—will also escape the judgment phase of the Day of the Lord when it finally does arrive.

In order to understand the nature of this prediction we must consider its fulfillment, then look back at its content.

Simon Peter declared that Joel's prophecy was fulfilled on the day of Pentecost.

> But Peter, standing up with the eleven, lifted up his voice, and spake forth unto them, saying, Ye men of Judea, and all ye that dwell at Jerusalem, be this known unto you, and give ear unto my words. For these are not drunken, as ye suppose; seeing it is but the third hour of the day; but this is that which hath been spoken through the prophet Joel (Ac 2:14-16).

Then the apostle Peter quoted Joel 2:28-32, "And it shall be in the last days, saith God, I will pour forth my Spirit upon all flesh" (Ac 2:17). Joel said "afterward." Simon Peter said, "in the last days." The apostle, under the inspiration of the Holy Spirit, was giving the sense of Joel's prophecy, for the words "in the last days" do not appear in the Old Testament text of Joel 2:28, neither in the Hebrew (MT) nor in the Greek (LXX). Peter was interpreting what Joel meant by "afterward." He affirmed that Joel's "afterward" is to be located in "the last days."

We tend to think of "the last days" as referring to that time immediately preceding the second coming of Christ. However, the New Testament indicates that "the last days" comprise the entire period extending between the first and the second advents of the Lord Jesus Christ. Dr. Carver says,

> "The last days" were the days of judgment and of the Messiah. These days had now come. They continue through all the gospel age, to full consummation at the close of this age. Peter did not define, and probably he had little thought of their being lengthened into centuries.[7]

Pentecost *fulfills* Joel's prediction about the coming of the Spirit. It does not *exhaust* it, however.

Since "the last days" cover the entire age of the Church, the Spirit is still being poured out upon individuals who repent and believe the Gospel. This will continue until the Church age ends at the rapture. Then Joel's prophecy will find its ultimate fulfillment at the close of the Tribulation period when the Spirit is poured out upon the nation Israel. This is why Joel's words about the coming of the Spirit (Ac 2:17-18), and his apocalyptic prediction (Ac 2:19-20), and his promise of salvation (Ac 2:21) will all be fulfilled in "the last days." These days stretch from Pentecost in the first century A.D., through the age of the Church, until the second coming of Christ.

Therefore Joel's prediction has *initial* fulfillment at Pentecost, *continuing* fulfillment during the Church age, and *ultimate* fulfillment at the second coming of Christ.

"This is that" said Simon Peter in his Pentecostal sermon (2:16) as he identified what had just happened with the fulfillment of Joel's prophecy. Luke, the writer of Acts, described what had just taken place, saying,

> And when the day of Pentecost was now come, they were all together in one place. And suddenly there came from heaven a sound as of the rushing of a mighty wind, and it filled all the house where they were sitting. And there appeared unto them tongues parting asunder, like as of fire;

and it sat upon each one of them. And they were all filled
with the Holy Spirit, and began to speak with other tongues,
as the Spirit gave them utterance (Ac 2:1-4).

Why was this day—the Jewish feast of Pentecost—chosen
for the initial fulfillment of Joel's prophecy?

"Pentecost," a term adopted from the Greek, means "fiftieth." Though the word Pentecost does not appear in the Old
Testament, or in the gospels—where the feast itself is not
mentioned—it does appear in Acts 2:1; 20:16; and 1 Corin-
thians 16:8. In the Old Testament the feast is called by various names, such as the "feast of weeks," Exodus 34:22; Deuteronomy 16:10; 2 Chronicles 8:13; "feast of harvest," Exodus
23:16; "day of the firstfruits," Numbers 28:26; Exodus 23:
16; 34:22.

The feast of Pentecost occurs fifty days after Passover. It was
originally an agricultural feast. On that day the Jews expressed gratitude to God for the return from their labors in
the fields. However, the Jews of Jesus' time had a second
view. They believed that Pentecost celebrated the giving of
the Law at Sinai which was calculated to have taken place on
the fiftieth day after the Exodus. This interpretation of Pentecost is not found in the Old Testament, however. But the
early Church Fathers accepted this as the meaning of Pentecost. So do modern Jews.

The Old Testament does not give the feast of Pentecost
the prominence that later Jewish writers do. But by the time
of Christ it had become an important feast, commemorating
the giving of the Law at Mount Sinai. It is this idea—accepted
by both Jews of the first century and the Church Fathers—
which enhances the meaning of the coming of the Spirit on
that day. Just as the Jewish feast of Pentecost celebrated the
giving of the outward Law at Sinai, so the Pentecostal coming
of the Holy Spirit celebrates the giving of the inward Law.
The Spirit comes to take the Law, previously written on tab-

lets of stone, and write it upon the heart of the born-again believer. Though Joel did not see this particular work of the Holy Spirit, the prophets Jeremiah (31:31-34) and Ezekiel (36:26-28) did. Joel predicted the fact of the outpouring of the Spirit. These later prophets interpreted its meaning.

What Jeremiah and Ezekiel said about the new heart is also capable of dual fulfillment. It is being fulfilled in the present Church age when individual sinners among the Gentiles are receiving the new heart. It will also have ultimate fulfillment when the nation Israel is given a new heart at the second coming of Christ, according to the literal application of both Jeremiah's and Ezekiel's words. Thus their predictions were primarily directed to Israel and Judah; however, according to the writer of the book of Hebrews (8:8-12), the promise of the new heart is also realized in the Church.

The promise of Joel found initial fulfillment when the day of Pentecost was fully come. But this did not deplete the content of Joel's great prediction. His prophecy is to experience a perpetual fulfillment during all the age of the Church.

Beginning at Pentecost, the Spirit has come upon people, both Jews and Gentiles, who have repented and received the Lord Jesus Christ as personal Saviour. He will continue to do so until the rapture. At Pentecost the Spirit came upon individual believers who make up the Church, the Body of Christ. But in each new generation the Spirit also comes upon those individuals who repent and believe the Gospel. Just as Calvary is a historical event, the benefits of which must be personally appropriated in the experience of every individual who is saved, so the historical benefits of Pentecost must also be personally experienced. This is not by a separate act of faith, by the way, but as a part of the total salvation experience. The Spirit came to indwell the Church for the first time on the day of Pentecost. But He continues to come to each new believer, in each successive generation, in order to indwell that believer also. This process which began at Pentecost will continue until the Body of Christ is completed. When the final sinner who is to make up the Church repents and receives Jesus as personal Saviour, the Holy Spirit will baptize that believer into the Body of Christ. Then the rapture will occur. The Church, in whom the Spirit dwells, will be caught out to meet the Lord Jesus in the air, and this phase of the fufillment of Joel's prophecy will end.

Pentecost is the initial fulfillment of Joel's prophecy. Now the Church age is witnessing its continuing fulfillment. But the ultimate fulfillment of Joel's prophecy about the Spirit is still to come.

While the Church participates in the continuing fulfillment of Joel's prophecy, the Holy Spirit is yet to be poured out upon Israel nationally. The promise was first made to Israel. It will ultimately be fulfilled in the nation, God's covenant people Israel.

Today Israel is returning to the land—still in unbelief. In 1948 the second exile ended. At the same time the Church, the Body of Christ, is being brought to completion. When it is completed, the Church will be taken out of the world. Then God will begin again to deal with Israel in the land.

Just after the rapture of the Church, the Antichrist will come upon the world scene as head of the revived Roman Empire. Israel will become a province of Rome, as it was in the first century when the prophetic time clock stopped at the end of Daniel's sixty-ninth week. Israel has one more week—seven years—which is to run its course. Daniel declared,

> Seventy weeks are decreed upon thy people and upon thy holy city, to finish transgression, and to make an end of sins, and to make reconciliation for iniquity, and to bring in everlasting righteousness, and to seal up vision and prophecy, and anoint the most holy (Dan 9:24) .

During the first part of this final seven-year period, Israel will dwell safely in the land under the protection of the Antichrist. The Temple will be rebuilt and the sacrifices will be made again after nearly twenty centuries. Israel may suspect that her golden age has arrived. But at mid-Tribulation the peace will be shattered, the sacrifices stopped, and the Temple will be desecrated by the image of the beast. Israel will be plunged into her final holocaust. For the next three and a half years the Jews will know only unprecedented horror. Jeremiah called this the time of Jacob's trouble, saying,

> We have heard a voice of trembling, of fear, and not of peace. Ask ye now, and see whether a man doth travail with child: wherefore do I see every man with his hands on his loins, as a woman in travail, and all faces are turned into paleness? Alas! For that day is great, so that none is like it: it is even the time of Jacob's trouble; but he shall be saved out of it. And it shall come to pass in that day, saith the LORD of hosts, that I will break his yoke from off his neck, and will burst thy bonds; and strangers shall no more make him their bondman; but they shall serve the LORD their God, and David their king, whom I will raise up unto them (Jer 30:5-9).

Jesus called this the time of Great Tribulation, declaring, "For then shall be great tribulation, such as hath not been from the beginning of the world until now, no, nor ever shall be" (Mt 24:21).

The Talmud says, "Why is Israel like an olive? As the olive gives its oil only by being crushed, so does Israel repent only through chastisements."[8] This crushing time of Great Tribulation for Israel is designed, in the providence of God, to prepare Israel for her coming Messiah. When the Lord Jesus Christ comes the second time, a faithful remnant in Israel will receive Him as Messiah. Those Jews who do so will be regenerated. In addition they will receive the Spirit. The Talmud also says, "Israel is like a vine: trodden under foot; but some time later its wine is placed on the table of a king. So, Israel, at first oppressed, will eventually come to greatness."[9] When they do, Joel's prophecy will find its ideal fulfillment.

This is how the other prophets envisioned the fulfillment of Joel's prediction which ultimately will take place at the second coming of Christ:

> Upon the land of my people shall come up thorns and briers; yea, upon all the houses of joy in the joyous city: for the palace shall be forsaken; the populous city shall be deserted; the hill and the watch-tower shall be for dens for ever, a joy of wild asses, a pasture of flocks; until the Spirit be poured upon us from on high, and the wilderness become a fruitful field, and the fruitful field be esteemed as a forest (Is 32:13-15).

> Fear not, O Jacob my servant; and thou Jeshurun, whom I have chosen. For I will pour water upon him that is thirsty, and streams upon the dry ground; I will pour my Spirit upon thy seed, and my blessing upon thine offspring (Is 44:2-3).

> Thus saith the LORD God: I will gather you from the peoples, and assemble you out of the countries where ye have been scattered, and I will give you the land of Israel. And they shall come thither, and they shall take away all the detestable things thereof and all the abominations thereof from thence. And I will give them one heart, and I will put a new spirit within you (Eze 11:16-17).

> And I will put my Spirit within you, and cause you to walk in my statutes, and ye shall keep mine ordinances, and do them. And ye shall dwell in the land that I gave to your fathers; and ye shall be my people, and I will be your God (Eze 36:27-28).

> Behold, I will open your graves, and cause you to come up out of your graves, O my people; and I will bring you into the land of Israel. And ye shall know that I am the LORD, when I have opened your graves, and caused you to come up out of your graves, O my people. And I will put my Spirit in you, and ye shall live, and I will place you in your own land: and ye shall know that I, the LORD, have

spoken it and performed it, saith the LORD (Eze 37:12-14) .

And they shall know that I am the LORD their God, in that I caused them to go into captivity among the nations, and have gathered them up unto their own land; and I will leave none of them any more there; neither will I hide my face any more from them; for I have poured out my Spirit upon the house of Israel, saith the LORD God (Eze 39:28-29) .

It is significant that each of these predictions about the Spirit's outpouring upon Israel has one thing in common. They all insist that the outpouring of the Spirit takes place in the land. When it occurs, the prophets also insist that this coming of the Spirit will have healing effects upon the land. The land will experience the physical benefits of fertility and security as a result of the advent of the Spirit upon the people.

What Joel envisioned 2,800 years ago was fulfilled in the first century at Pentecost. Yet it is still being fulfilled as the born-again believer, in each successive generation of the Church age, receives the Spirit. But further fulfillment awaits. Israel nationally is to receive the Spirit when the covenant people accept Jesus as Messiah and Saviour at His second coming.

All of this complex Pentecostal and eschatological fulfillment is found in the prophet's words:

> And it shall come to pass afterward, that I will pour out my Spirit upon all flesh; and your sons and your daughters shall prophesy, your old men shall dream dreams, your young men shall see visions: and also upon the servants and upon the handmaids in those days will I pour out my Spirit (Joel 2:28-29) .

Joel's prediction has two features. The first one is his startling revelation about who is to receive the Spirit. The Spirit will come upon "all flesh," affirmed Joel. This includes sons, daughters, old men, young men, servants, and handmaids.

Are all these people Jews? Or is "all flesh" a universal term?

Rabbi Ibn Ezra says that "all flesh" refers only to those Jews who live in the land of Israel, for they alone are fit to receive the visitation of the divine Spirit. In contrast to this Jewish provincialism, the New Testament universalizes the promise. Simon Peter said, "For to you is the promise, and to your children, and all that are afar off, even as many as the Lord our God shall call unto him" (Ac 2:39). Those "afar off" are Gentiles (Eph 2:13, 17). Acts 10:45 is conclusive, declaring that Gentiles are included in the promise, "And they of the circumcision that believed were amazed, as many as came with Peter, because that on the Gentiles also was poured out the gift of the Holy Spirit."

Moses said, "Would that all the LORD's people were prophets, that the LORD would put his Spirit upon them!" (Num 11:29). Joel declared that the day is coming when Moses' wish for the people will be fulfilled. All the Lord's people will receive the Spirit. However, Joel's universalism was a little too much for later Jewish commentators. The prophet declared, "And also." A better translation would be, "And even upon the servants and upon the handmaids in those days will I pour out my Spirit." However, when the Jewish translators of the Septuagint came to this passage, they rendered it, "my servants" and "my handmaids" (servants and handmaids of God and not of men). This reflects the Jew's reluctance to concede that even slaves—and what is more sensational, women— will receive the Spirit! But this is just what the prophet Joel was declaring. The Spirit will be universally given; Gentiles will receive the Spirit, and so will the lowly slave. But, to the Jewish reader, something more startling than Joel's promise to slaves is his assertion that even women are included in the blessing.

The second feature of Joel's prediction comprises the results of the outpouring of the Spirit. These results are couched in terms of prophetic utterance. The traditional forms of prophetic revelation—dreams and visions—are here. God said to Moses, "Hear now my words: if there be a prophet among you, I the LORD will make myself known unto him in a vision, I will speak with him in a dream" (Num 12:6). Joel's prediction was that in the day of the Spirit everyone would be his own prophet. All would have a direct revelation from God. Jeremiah confirmed this in his prediction about the new covenant, saying, "And they shall teach no more every man his neighbor, and every man his brother, saying, Know the LORD; for they shall all know me, from the least of them unto the greatest of them, saith the LORD" (Jer 31:34). They said that when the Holy Spirit would be outpoured, this would equip everyone to have a direct and personal experience with God.

While this idea is commonplace to us, in ancient Israel it was a profound promise. In those days there were two intermediaries between God and Israel: the prophet, who represented God to the people; and the priest, who represented the people to God. But, said Joel, there was a day coming when neither prophet nor priest would be necessary, for each individual would have his own personal encounter with God through the Holy Spirit.

At Pentecost the disciples—previously justified by faith, as were all the Old Testament saints—were brought into this new and dramatic personal encounter with God through the Holy Spirit.

First, the disciples were regenerated. By this work of the Spirit, Christ is placed in the believer.

Second, the disciples were baptized by the Spirit into the Body of Christ. This places the believer in Christ. The consequence of this twofold operation of the Spirit is that the believer is now in Christ, and Christ is now in the believer. A more intimate and profound encounter between God and man cannot be imagined. Nothing could be more intimate than Christ in you, and you in Christ.

Third, the believer is made a member of the family of God by the Holy Spirit. One is born into the family of God by regeneration, a work of the Spirit. In addition, the believer is adopted into the family of God, also a work of the Spirit. Added to the dynamic terms of "regeneration" and the "baptism of the Spirit" is the domestic term of intimacy within the family of God. The Spirit makes us "sons of God" by faith in Christ.

Fourth, the disciple is sealed in this relationship. Eternally secure in the family of God is the believer to whom the Spirit comes.

Fifth, the Holy Spirit fills the disciple, producing in him the fruit of love out of which emerges all the attributes of God.

All of these are the believer's heritage because the Holy Spirit has been poured upon him, resulting in this profound and personal experience with God, as Joel predicted. It began at Pentecost. It will continue in each succeeding generation until the Church, the Body of Christ, is completed and then caught out of the world at the rapture.

After this, the Spirit will be outpoured upon the nation Israel, bringing each individual Jewish believer into this personal encounter with God also.

The day of the Spirit—stretching between Pentecost and the second coming of Christ—affects both Gentiles in the Church and Jews in covenant. It is the alternative to the Day of the Lord.

Which of these days prevails depends upon the people. If they repent, the day of the Spirit is their alternative. If they do not, the Day of the Lord is inevitable.

5

THE ARRIVAL OF THE DAY OF THE LORD

Joel 3:1-17

THE APOSTLE PETER declared,

> But forget not this one thing, beloved, that one day is with the Lord as a thousand years, and a thousand years as one day. The Lord is not slack concerning his promise, as some count slackness; but is longsuffering to you-ward, not wishing that any should perish, but that all should come to repentance. But the day of the Lord will come (2 Pe 3:8-10).

The long-suffering of God and the repentance of the people served to delay the Day of the Lord down through the centuries. "But," said Peter, "the day of the Lord will come!" It cannot be averted indefinitely.

When will it come? Joel had the answer.

In fact, his basic inquiry concerning the Day of the Lord not only supplies the *when* of the day, but also the other components of the journalistic theme: the *what, where,* and *why* of the day.

When will the Day of the Lord arrive?

Upon what—or whom—will it come?

Where will it occur?

Why will it fall upon whom it does?

Transparent as this literary format might be, it is apparent in the first two verses of chapter 3, where the prophet says,

> For, behold, in those days, and in that time, when I shall bring back the captivity of Judah and Jerusalem, I will gather all nations, and will bring them down into the valley of Jehoshaphat; and I will execute judgment upon them there for my people and for my heritage Israel, whom they have scattered among the nations: and they have parted my land (Joel 3:1-2).

At what point in human history does the Day of the Lord finally arrive? Joel's dateline for the day is when the Lord "shall bring back the captivity of Judah and Jerusalem."

The two events—Israel's return from exile, and the Day of the Lord upon the nations—are interrelated. Therefore the return must involve more than a modern Zionist initiative. This aspiration is both an objective fact in biblical prophecy and a fundamental trait of Jewishness. Following the Six Day War in 1967, General Charles de Gaulle castigated the Jews as "an aggressive people." David Ben Gurion wrote him, pointing out an obvious fact of history, saying "No other people has been so exiled, despised, hated, persecuted, harried from country to country and finally (in our own time and in supposedly civilized Europe) slaughtered *en masse*. During all this," said Ben Gurion, "we neither vanished nor despaired, nor assimilated, but held fast to the conviction that we would some day regain our land."[1] Israel's passion for the land is not the result of Jewish aggressiveness, but of a divinely implanted impulse within the Jewish heart.

Judah's return from exile sets the stage for the Day of the Lord. The day cannot come until Israel is back in the land.

Historically, this prerequisite has been fulfilled only one time: at the close of the Babylonian Exile in the sixth century B.C. However, it is obvious that the Day of the Lord did not occur at this time, for the dominion of the Gentiles over Israel was not broken. Judah returned to Eretz Israel, the land of Israel. However, they remained under Gentile determination.

After the first Exile, the Jews were restored to the land, but they were then successively ruled by Persians, Greeks—both Ptolemies and Seleucids—and finally by the Romans.

Then another exile began in A.D. 70.

This exile was to extend for nearly 2,000 years into the future. It ended in 1948.

During all of this vast period of time—from the Babylonian conquest until today, already 2,600 years—the Jews have been under Gentile control. Jesus called this era "the times of the Gentiles" (Lk 21:24). These times began with Judah's first Gentile overlords, the Babylonians. The time of the Gentiles is still running its course, for Israel's destiny is to this day determined by the nations and not by the Jews themselves. The Babylonians, Persians, Greeks, and Romans dictated Israel's fortunes between 587 B.C. and A.D. 70. This determination continued through the following 1,878 years of exile.

In 1948 the Jewish state was created by the United Nations partition of Palestine. Even then the Old City of Jerusalem remained in the hands of the Jordanians. It was not until the Six Day War of 1967 that Israel became sovereign over much of her former territory, including the Old City.

However, the basic insecurity of the Jewish state was later to be demonstrated during the Yom Kippur War in October, 1973. Egypt and Syria attacked Israel on her most holy day, the Day of Atonement. At first, the Arabs made some military advances. Egypt regained some territory east of the Suez Canal in the Sinai Desert. Syria penetrated into her former territory, now held by Israel, on the Golan Heights. But, within a matter of days, Israel's military forces began to penetrate northeast toward Damascus and southwest into Egypt itself. Israel gained new territory west of Suez. Then the United Nations, backed by the United States and Russia, forced a cease fire in the Middle East. Israel later returned some captured territory to the Arabs. The final truce arrangements were due largely to the work of United States Secretary of State, Henry Kissinger.

Following the struggle, the influence of the United States and Soviet Union dictated Israel's fate. It was the United States which negotiated peace between Arabs and Jews. What territory the Jews gave up to the Arabs was conceived by the United States to be in the general interest of peace in the Middle East, and not primarily for Israel's own interests. Because Israel was dependent upon the Americans for the resupply of arms, she was forced to do their bidding.

This is but a further indication that Israel is still under Gentile dominion. The resolve of the nations, not the Jews themselves, still gives the current verdict to Israel's history. Though this political determinism is more subtle than the Gentiles' former physical dominion over the Jews, it is evidence that the times of the Gentiles have not ended. The nations still decree Israel's destiny.

Joel said that only the Day of the Lord can reverse this situation. It will be the Day of the Lord which finally and conclusively breaks Gentile dominion over Israel.

Joel also affirmed that Israel must be in the land before this can occur. The Day of the Lord can only come when "I shall bring back the captivity of Judah and Jerusalem," saith the Lord. Therefore, the nation Israel is God's prophetic timepiece. If you wish to know where we are in the prophetic program of God, watch Israel. The nation is the frame of reference for all predictive prophecy. God's dealing with the Church is a mystery, to use Paul's term (Eph 3:3-11). It occurs within a great intermission in God's dealing with Israel, a parenthesis which is interposed between Pentecost and the rapture. There is no Old Testament prediction about the course of the Church age. In fact, the Church is never seen by the Old Testament prophets. But God's dealing with the nation Israel is overt. Israel is the sign to all the world concerning the movement of God in history and prophecy.

The Old Testament predicts both scattering and regathering for Israel. Scattering from off the land is Israel's unique punishment for sin. Regathering back to the land is God's unique covenant promise to His people. Both are an important part of God's program for Israel.

Moses called these alternatives "the blessing and the curse" (Deu 30:1).

The Talmud says, "Woe to the children, for whose sins I destroyed My house, burnt My temple, and exiled My people among the nations! Woe to the father who had to banish his children, and woe to the children who had to be banished from their father's table!"[2] The Midrash explains that "exile is as hard as all other punishments combined."[3] And yet, Israel knew that exile and scattering were to be the Jews' singular punishment for sin. The Torah warns of this. So do the writings and the prophets.

One of the clearest warnings that forfeiture of the land will result from Israel's sin is found in Moses' first address while on the plain of Moab. The people had only recently come out of Egypt. They were about to go into the land. Moses said,

> When thou shalt beget children, and children's children, and ye shall have been long in the land, and shall corrupt yourselves, and make a graven image in the form of any thing, and shall do that which is evil in the sight of the LORD thy God, to provoke him to anger; I call heaven and earth to witness against you this day, that ye shall soon utterly perish from off the land whereunto ye go over Jordan to possess it; ye shall not prolong your days upon it, but shall utterly be destroyed. And the LORD will scatter you among the peoples, and ye shall be left few in number among the nations, whither the LORD shall lead you away (Deu 4:25-27).

The former prophets said,

> For the LORD will smite Israel, as a reed is shaken in the water; and he will root up Israel out of this good land which

he gave to their fathers, and will scatter them beyond the River, because they have made their Asherim, provoking the LORD to anger (1 Ki 14:15).

Hosea, a latter Hebrew prophet, said, "My God will cast them away, because they did not harken unto him; and they shall be wanderers among the nations" (Ho 9:17).

The psalmist lamented, "Thou hast made us like sheep appointed for food, and hast scattered us among the nations" (Ps 44:11). Recalling Moses' address, the psalmist said, "Therefore, he sware unto them, that he would overthrow them in the wilderness, and that he would overthrow their seed among the nations, and scatter them in the lands" (Ps 106:26-27).

So keenly did the Jew feel this punishment that the rabbis, writing in the Talmud, said, "Exile atones for everything."[4]

However, Israel's lamentation during the Exile was not without hope. In fact, Zechariah called Israel in Exile, "prisoners of hope" (9:12). The Hebrew word for this hope is *hatikvah*. This is also the name of Israel's national anthem, which is translated as follows:

> So long as still within our breasts
> The Jewish heart beats true,
> So long as still towards the East,
> To Zion, looks the Jew,
> So long our hopes are not yet lost—
> Two thousand years we cherished them—
> To live in freedom in the land
> Of Zion and Jerusalem.

The book of Tobit was written around the second century B.C. Its setting, however, is in the eighth century B.C. when Israel fell to the Assyrians and the Northern Kingdom went into exile. The book expresses *hatikvah*—the hope—as Tobit, a devout Jew in exile, said that

our brethren shall lie scattered in the earth from that good

land: and Jerusalem shall be desolate, and the house of God
in it shall be burned, and shall be desolate for a time; and
that again God will have mercy on them, and bring them
again into the land, where they shall build a temple, and
not like to the first, until the time of that age be fulfilled;
and afterward they shall return from all places of their captivity, and build up Jerusalem gloriously, and the house of
God shall be built in it for ever with a glorious building, as
the prophets have spoken thereof (Tobit 14:4-5).

The writer of this apocryphal book tells us the source of this
hope, "the prophets have spoken thereof."

They have done so quite clearly. Therefore their words
about the restoration of Israel should not only be taken seriously, but also literally.

Moses wrote, "And the Lord thy God will bring thee into
the land which thy fathers possessed, and thou shalt possess
it" (Deu 30:5).

Isaiah declared,

> And it shall come to pass in that day, that the Lord will
> set his hand again the second time to recover the remnant
> of his people, that shall remain (11:11).
>
> And ye shall be gathered one by one, O ye children of
> Israel (27:12).
>
> I will bring thy seed from the east, and gather thee from
> the west; I will say to the north, Give up; and to the south,
> Keep not back; bring my sons from far, and my daughters
> from the end of the earth (43:5-6).
>
> For a small moment have I forsaken thee; but with great
> mercies will I gather thee (54:7).
>
> The Lord God who gathereth the outcasts of Israel (56:8).

Amos affirmed,

> And I will bring back the captivity of my people Israel,
> and they shall build the waste cities, and inhabit them. . . .
> And I will plant them upon their land, and they shall no

more be plucked up out of their land which I have given
them, saith the LORD thy God (9:14-15).

Micah decreed,

In that day, saith the LORD, will I assemble that which is
lame, and I will gather that which is driven away, and that
which I have afflicted; and I will make that which was lame a
remnant, and that which was cast far off a strong nation:
and the LORD will reign over them in mount Zion from
henceforth even for ever (4:6-7).

Jeremiah bore witness, saying,

And it shall come to pass, after that I have plucked them
up, I will return and have compassion on them; and I will
bring them again, every man to his heritage, and every man
to his land (12:15).

O LORD, save thy people, the remnant of Israel. Behold,
I will bring them from the north country, and gather them
from the uttermost parts of the earth . . . a great company
shall they return hither (31:7-8).

Behold, I will gather them out of all the countries, whither
I have driven them in mine anger, and in my wrath, and in
great indignation; and I will bring them again unto this
place, and I will cause them to dwell safely (32:37).

Ezekiel related how God

will gather you from the peoples, and assemble you out of
the countries where ye have been scattered, and I will give
you the land of Israel (11:17).

When I shall have gathered the house of Israel from the
peoples among whom they are scattered . . . then shall they
dwell in their own land which I gave to my servant Jacob
(28:25).

So will I seek out my sheep; and I will deliver them out of
all places whither they have been scattered in the cloudy and
dark day. And I will bring them out from the peoples, and

gather them from the countries, and will bring them into their land (34:12-13).

Behold, I will open their graves, and cause you to come up out of your graves, O my people; and I will bring you into the land of Israel (37:12).

Zephaniah promised,

At that time will I bring you in, and at that time will I gather you; for I will make you a name and a praise among all the peoples of the earth when I bring back your captivity before your eyes, saith the LORD (3:20).

Many of these passages found partial fulfillment when the Jews were returned from the Babylonian Exile. However, the results of this restoration in the sixth century B.C. never realized the glorious fulfillment envisioned by the prophets. Therefore, what the prophets saw is reserved for a later time, yet future.

There was a second exile, beginning with the fall of the second Temple in A.D. 70.

There will also be a second regathering from exile, as Isaiah predicted (11:11). Only after this full return from the second exile will the vision of the prophets be fulfilled in restored Israel.

Are we witnessing the beginning of this restoration today? Is it prophetically significant that for the first time in nearly 2,000 years there is a state of Israel?

Obviously the Israel of today is no theocracy such as the prophets envisioned. The late David Ben Gurion, Israel's first prime minister, was an agnostic, if not an atheist. In his memoirs he speaks of himself as "one who is non-religious." He also admits that "as a boy I suddenly declared my disbelief in God."[5] Subsequent prime ministers have been more or less religious. None of them were observant, that is, neither Moshe Sharett, Levi Eshkol, nor Golda Meir regarded the kosher tenets of orthodox Judaism. General Moshe Dayan has observed that Israel "is the fulfillment of a militant Jewishness that transcends religion." Religion has never been an issue among Israel's national figures, for the people indicate no concern at this time for a theocratic kingdom in Israel.

However, this should not come as a surprise. The prophets not only predicted the restoration of Israel, but they also indicated that this restoration would begin while the people were still under the sentence of judicial blindness (Ro 11:25). Though a repentant attitude may prevail even while they are outside the land in exile (Deu 30:2), their spiritual regeneration will not occur until they are back in the land. Therefore, their initial regathering is predicted to occur while the Jews are yet in unbelief.

This is what we are witnessing today.

Further indications are that their unbelief will continue until the second coming of Christ. Though many indvidual Jews will be saved during the Tribulation period, Israel nationally will not be spiritually redeemed until the Messiah comes.

The most telling indication that the national tenure of Israel during the Tribulation will be one of unbelief is the covenant which is sustained between the nation and the Antichrist (Dan 9:27). Under this covenant the Temple will be rebuilt and the Levitical sacrifices resumed. It will not be until the close of the Tribulation that the remnant which represents faithful Israel will accept Jesus as Messiah and the covenant people will be regenerated.

Therefore the things which are taking place in Israel today are prophetically significant only in that they are setting the stage for the events of the Tribulation period. These events will lead up to the national acceptance of Jesus as Messiah when He comes again.

Will this current regathering of the people be sustained? Can the State of Israel, having observed its silver anniversary in 1973, continue? Or will it be forced out of existence by the Arabs? Will the Jews ever again suffer exile and deportation from the land?

There is nothing inherent in this present stage of prophetic development to guarantee that Israel will survive as a nation. However, if what we are witnessing today is in truth *the* regathering prior to the Tribulation, then nothing will interfere with God's program for Israel during the closing days of the Church age which lead up to the Tribulation period.

In addition, there is an intransigent nationalism current among repatriated Jews which will admit no compromise. There are only two alternatives. With the Jews in Israel today it is either possession of the land or annihilation. This inflexible mandate to stay in the land was delivered on October 7, 1957, to the whole world. Golda Meir, then foreign minister of Israel, laid aside her prepared text, as she spoke before the General Assembly of the United Nations, and said,

> From the rostrum I should like to address a solemn appeal to the Arab states of the Middle East: Israel is approaching her tenth anniversary. You did not want it to be born. You fought against the decision in the United Nations. You then attacked us by military force. We have all been witnesses to sorrow, destruction, and the spilling of blood and tears. Yet Israel is here, growing, developing, progressing. It has gained many friends, and their number is steadily increasing. We are an old tenacious people and, as our history has proved, not easily destroyed. Like you, the Arab countries, we have regained our national independence, and as with you, so with us, nothing will cause us to give it up. We are here to stay. History has decreed that the Middle East consists of an independent Israel and independent Arab states. This verdict will never be reversed.[6]

Israel is back in the land and determined to stay. The Jews have declared, "Masada will not fall again!" The people will never again capitulate to the nations if they try to force her from the land. This the Romans did 2,000 years ago. It will not happen another time. Israel may have to make periodic adjustments in the territory she possesses, as she did following the Yom Kippur War. But never will world Jewry permit itself to become what it was prior to 1948. As far as human determination is concerned, Israel is in the land to stay.

And with this determination, Joel's first prerequisite for the Day of the Lord has been fulfilled. It will occur, he said, "in those days, and in that time, when I shall bring back the captivity of Judah and Jerusalem" (Joel 3:1).

Joel also indicated upon whom the Day of the Lord is to come. He says, "I will gather all nations, and will bring them down into the valley of Jehoshaphat; and I will execute judgment upon them there" (3:2).

The Day of the Lord could have fallen upon Judah in the prophet's own time if the people had not repented and averted the day.

Now it is to come upon Israel's enemies, the nations.

The Great Midrash says that Abraham warned his sons by Keturah never to come near Isaac and his descendants until the advent of the Messiah. "Because," said Abraham, "any nation ruling over the Jews will suffer the punishment of Gehenna."[7] Joel lent substance to this Midrash when he indicated that the Day of the Lord will fall upon the Gentile nations because of what they have done to Israel.

The Day of the Lord is to come upon the nations. It will occur during the Great Tribulation period, for one objective of the Tribulation period is to punish the nations (Is 26:21; 2 Th 2:12; Rev 3:10). Israel will also be involved in the Great Tribulation. This is "the time of Jacob's trouble" (Jer 30:7), and its intent for Israel is to prepare the nation for the coming of Jesus, Israel's Messiah. However, this will be a time of national deliverance for Israel. The people, at least a faithful remnant, will be saved in the Day of the Lord just as they were in Joel's day. And by the same recourse, that is, repentance (Zec 12:10). This Joel affirmed in 2:30-32,

> And I will show wonders in the heavens and in the earth: blood, and fire, and pillars of smoke. The sun shall be turned into darkness, and the moon into blood, before the great and terrible day of the LORD cometh. And it shall come to pass, that whosoever shall call on the name of the LORD shall be delivered; for in mount Zion and in Jerusalem there shall be those that escape, as the LORD hath said, and among the remnant those whom the LORD doth call.

The prophet Malachi is even more specific than is Joel. He indicated that it would be at the preaching of Elijah that this turning would occur. Elijah will be to the Tribulation Jews what Joel was to the Hebrews in his day, or what John the Baptist was to the Jews of his day.

> Behold, I will send you Elijah the prophet before the great and terrible day of the LORD come. And he shall turn the heart of the fathers to the children, and the heart of the children to their fathers; lest I come and smite the earth with a curse (Mal 4:5-6).

Elijah will perform this ministry of reconciliation between the nation Israel and God when he appears as one of the two witnesses of Revelation 11. His ministry will extend the length of the Great Tribulation (Rev 11:3).

The nations upon whom the Day of the Lord will fall are those who have persecuted Israel. These Gentile persecutors have been represented by various nations in the past. For example, in the book of Obadiah the Edomites are the archpersecutors of Israel. Upon them the Day of the Lord will come. Obadiah says,

> For the day of the LORD is near upon all the nations: as thou [Edom] hast done, it shall be done unto thee; thy dealing shall return upon thine own head.
>
> Shall I not in that day, saith the LORD, destroy the wise men out of Edom, and understanding out of the mount of Esau? And thy mighty men, O Teman, shall be dismayed, to the end that every one may be cut off from the mount of

> Esau by slaughter. For the violence done to thy brother Jacob, shame shall cover thee, and thou shalt be cut off for ever (Ob 15, 8-10).

In Isaiah's day it was the Babylonians upon whom the day was to come.

> Wail ye [Babylonians]; for the day of the Lord is at hand; as destruction from the Almighty shall it come. Behold, the day of the Lord cometh, cruel, with wrath and fierce anger; to make the land a desolation, and to destroy the sinners thereof out of it (Is 13:6, 9).

Jeremiah saw the Day of the Lord coming upon Egypt. He said, "For that day is a day of the Lord, the Lord of hosts, a day of vengeance, that he may avenge him of his adversaries: and the sword shall devour and be satiate, and shall drink its fill of their blood" (Jer 46:10).

Ezekiel also indicated that Egypt represented the enemies of the people of God upon whom the day is to fall. "Wail ye, Alas for the day! For the day is near, even the day of the Lord is near; it shall be a day of clouds, a time of the nations. And a sword shall come upon Egypt" (30:2-4).

In the Apocrypha Israel's traditional enemy was the Seleucid kingdom of Antiochus IV Epiphanes. In Daniel, Antiochus was actually presented as a type of the Antichrist, the final persecutor of Israel. In the Talmud Israel's traditional enemy was Rome. In the Midrash it was the four kingdoms—Babylon, Persia, Greece, and Rome. In the Inquisition it was the Roman Catholic Church. In the Zionist literature it was the Russians and their pograms. In the Holocaust literature it was the Nazis. Today it is the Arabs. In the book of Revelation it will be the earth dwellers, who make up the kingdom of the Antichrist, upon whom the wrath of God will fall during the Tribulation.

However, in the book of Joel it was the Phoenicians and the Philistines, enemies of the covenant people in that day, whom the prophet typed as the great persecutors of Israel. Upon them was the day to come (3:4-8), for they had been especially hostile to the Jews. Upon them the Day of the Lord will fall; however, they will be only the representatives of all those nations which have scattered and maltreated Israel. What is due the Phoenicians and the Philistines is also due for the Edomites, Egyptians, Babylonians, Persians, Greeks, Romans, Russians, Nazis, and Arabs—all who have persecuted the covenant people of God. This judgment, the Day of the Lord, will be historically realized during the Great Tribulation when it falls upon the kingdom of the Antichrist, the antitype of all the foes of Israel.

Though these nations were judged in their own time, there is also this final judgment reserved for the Gentile nations who are the end-time persecutors of Israel and who epitomize all the former enemies of the covenant people. This will occur toward the end of the Great Tribulation period, climaxing in the Battle of Armageddon. It is this judgment of the nations which is in view in Joel 3. Though he spoke of Israel's contemporary enemies, Tyre, Sidon, and Philistia, he saw beyond them to the actual Day of the Lord upon the nations which will occur just before the second coming of Christ.

What had the nations done to Israel? What was their specific crime which will condemn them on the Day of the Lord?

Joel was explicit. He declared,

> I will execute judgment upon them there for my people and for my heritage Israel, whom they have scattered among the nations: and they have parted my land, and have cast lots for my people, . . . ye have taken my silver and my gold, and have carried into your temples my goodly precious things (3:2-5).

The prophet indicated that the nations were guilty of four things which had been perpetrated upon Israel:

They had scattered Israel among the nations.

They had partitioned the Holy Land.

They had made slaves of the Jews.

They had carried away the sacred vessels of the Temple.

First, the nations deserve the Day of the Lord because they have scattered Israel.

Of course, the Bible also indicates that Israel was scattered as punishment for her own sin. The Talmud, Judah's oral law transcribed and commented upon, recognizes that the sin of Israel results in exile. The Talmud presents the Roman Empire as the traditional enemy of Israel and the agent of Israel's exile. Yet, paradoxically, it also indicates that the prosecutions of Rome are a result of Israel's own sin. One legend from the Talmud declares that the exile forced upon Israel by Rome was a direct result of the sin of Solomon which was perpetrated a thousand years before the fall of the second Temple.

> When King Solomon took Pharaoh's daughter for a wife she brought with her from Egypt a thousand different musical instruments. She instructed him in the use of all of them, saying, "In this manner you play to honor this idol, and in that manner you play to honor that idol." No word of reproach ever passed Solomon's lips. On that very day the angel Gabriel stuck a rod into the sea and around the rod formed sand and seaweed. From these arose an island and on the island was built the Empire of Rome which robbed the Jews of their land and drove them into exile.[8]

Though exile is ascribed to the sin of Israel, nevertheless the nations will suffer the Day of the Lord because they enforced this exile upon Israel.

In 721 B.C. the Northern Kingdom of Israel was scattered, never to return until the Messianic regathering occurs. In 587 B.C. the Southern Kingdom, Judah, was scattered. However, it was not until A.D. 70 that the great dispersion took place. This time Israel's scattering lasted for nearly two millenniums. In those ancient days the Gentile persecutors of

Israel were represented, in turn, by the Assyrians, the Babylonians, and the Romans. But in the end time all of these
Gentile nations will be summed up in the kingdom of the
Antichrist. Again Israel will be forced into exile. Jesus
warned that a final fleeing is impending for Israel. In His
prophetic discourse, uttered upon the Mount of Olives, He
said, "When therefore ye see the abomination of desolation,
which was spoken of through Daniel the prophet, standing in
the holy place (let him that readeth understand), then let
them that are in Judea flee unto the mountains" (Mt 24:15-
16).

However, this time Israel's scattering is not projected into
centuries of enforced wandering as it was between A.D. 70 and
1948. During this end-time fleeing, Israel will soon be rescued. The nations will be punished as the Day of the Lord
finally dawns, ushered in by the second coming of Christ.

The nations are guilty of a second crime against the sov-
ereignty of God; they have parted the Holy Land. Joel said,
"They have parted my land" (3:2).

The Assyrians did this. In an ancient Assyrian record, Sar-
gon II declared, "Samaria I besieged and took . . . 27,290 inhabitants I carried away . . . I set up again and made more
populous than before. People from other lands which I had
taken I settled there."[9] The Bible confirms this, saying,

> So Israel was carried away out of their own land to Assyria
> unto this day. And the king of Assyria brought men from
> Babylon, and from Cuthah, and from Avva, and from Ha-
> math and Sepharvaim, and placed them in the cities of
> Samaria instead of the children of Israel; and they possessed
> Samaria, and dwelt in the cities thereof (2 Ki 17:23-24).

These people became the Samaritans who in Jesus' day were
considered aliens in the land and enemies of the Jews. Both
the Roman General Titus and the Emperor Hadrian divided
the land after the Great Revolt of A.D. 70 and in the aftermath

of the Bar Kokhba Revolt of A.D. 135. Apparently the Antichrist will do the same thing, for Daniel says, "Whosoever acknowledgeth him he will increase with glory; and he shall cause them to rule over many, and shall divide the land for a price" (Dan 11:39). Once again the kingdom of the Antichrist epitomizes the history of Gentile encroachment upon the land which God gave to Israel.

Over and over again the nations have violated the covenant which God made with His people in which He granted to them the land (Gen 12:7; 13:15; 15:18-21; 17:8). This blasphemous usurpation of the prerogatives of God, who by sovereign decree granted the land to Israel, will not go unjudged. The Day of the Lord will deal with this sinful presumption of the nations in which they have divided the land God had given to Israel for all time.

The third offense which the nations committed against Israel, and for which they are destined to the Day of the Lord, is that they have made slaves of the Jews. Joel issued the indictment against the nations because they

> have cast lots for my people, and have given a boy for a harlot, and sold a girl for wine, that they may drink . . . and have sold the children of Judah and the children of Jerusalem unto the sons of the Grecians, that ye may remove them far from their border (3:3-6).

So little regard have the nations for Jewish dignity that a boy was bartered in payment to a harlot and a girl was exchanged for a bottle of wine. Joel's reference to these Greek slave traders has been taken as an indication of the late date of Joel. However, it is quite possible that slave trade was taking place between Greece and Tyre at this early day. The use of "Grecians" could easily refer, not to a nation, but to an isolated band of slave traders from a distant clime.[10]

Jews were sold as slaves during the Maccabean civil war. Antiochus's General Nicanor undertook to make so much money of the captive Jews, as should defray the tribute of two thousand talents, which the king was to pay to the Romans. Wherefore immediately he sent to the cities upon the sea coast, proclaiming a sale of the captive Jews, and promising that they should have fourscore and ten bodies for one talent, not expecting the vengeance that was to follow upon him from the Almighty God (2 Mac 8:10-11).

Titus also sold Jews into slavery after the Great Revolt. Josephus records that when Jerusalem fell, the soldiers of Titus became weary with killing Jews. Those who were not killed were shut up in the Temple before it was burned, and from

> the young men, he chose out the tallest and most beautiful, and reserved them for the triumph; and as for the rest of the multitude that were above seventeen years old, he put them into bonds, and sent them to the Egyptian mines. Titus also sent a great number into the provinces, as a present to them, that they might be destroyed upon their theaters, by the sword and by wild beasts; but those that were under seventeen years of age were sold for slaves.[11]

The Colosseum in Rome was built largely by the labor of Jewish slaves who were captured in the fall of Jerusalem in A.D. 70. When Hadrian finally put down the Bar Kokhba Revolt, so many Jews were sold into slavery that the slave markets were glutted. A horse was worth more than a human, so numerous were Jewish slaves in those days.

Finally, Joel indicated that the nations would experience the Day of the Lord because they had robbed the Jews of their treasures. Most commentators agree that the reference is to all the precious things in Judah, whether privately owned or the sacred vessels of the Temple. However, the Jewish commentators believe that "my goodly precious things" (3:5) refer to the Temple utensils.[12]

If we posit a ninth-century date for the book of Joel, the

Temple may not have been robbed at this time, though the city had been plundered (2 Ki 12:16; 2 Ch 21:16-17). However, the vision of Joel was predictive. He had the end time in view. The nations will be judged for each incident of Temple desecration, whether it occurred in 587 B.C., in 165 B.C., in A.D. 70, or during the Tribulation desecration of the Temple by the Antichrist.

The fate of the Temple vessels has given rise to a whole series of legends. In those legends the vessels of the first Temple were divinely protected. When the second Temple fell, the sacred vessels suffered an ignominious fate at the hands of their Gentile looters. This did not include the Ark of the Covenant, which was absent from the second Temple, having never been relocated after the destruction of Solmon's Temple in the sixth century B.C.

When the first Temple was destroyed, some Jews believe that the Ark of the Covenant merely sank into the ground. Others say that it lies hidden under the floor of the Lodge of Wood, that area of the Temple where the fuel for the sacrificial fires was stored. A priest, ministering in the second Temple, noted that a slab in the floor of this unroofed court was different from all the rest. He went to tell his fellow priests about it, but died on the way. This was a sure sign to the rabbis that the Ark of the Covenant must be hidden there. The Apocrypha says that the prophet Jeremiah hid the Ark on Mount Nebo and that the hiding place was lost because one of the prophet's students failed to mark the trail. It will be recovered when the Messiah comes, however.

Another legend says that when Solmon constructed the Temple, an ingenious concealment device for the Ark was developed. Knowing that the Temple would one day be destroyed, Solomon's architects designed a stone which would open in the Holy of Holies. Through this passage the Ark could be taken to concealment deep in the earth beneath Mount Moriah. There it remains today, sealed in the Well of Souls, which is below the foundation stone in the Dome of the Rock, says Jewish legend.

The disposition of the vessels of the second Temple are also surrounded with legend. Josephus says that Titus took them to Rome. The rabbis record that Titus made a basket out of the curtain which separated the Holy of Holies from the holy place and in this basket transported the vessels to Rome. Though the voyage was filled with peril, for the displeasure of God was upon this ship, the sacred vessels finally arrived at the empire's capital. In the second century A.D., Rabbi Yossi avows that he actually saw the holy curtain there. "Upon it were several drops of blood," he says. This reflects the tradition that Titus slashed the veil and that blood ran out.

The menorah was taken to Rome, where its picture appears on the Arch of Titus in the Forum. Later it was taken to Constantinople. Legend says that it was kindled and used in processions during Christian holidays as late as the tenth century A.D. It is also said that in the Great Dome, a cathedral in Prague, there is a candelabrum which was brought from Italy in 1158. Local legend affirms that this indeed is the Temple menorah. Rabbi Benjamine was in Rome in 1175. He declares that he saw pillars there which Titus had taken from the Temple. Each year on the Ninth of Av, the day in which Jews mourn the loss of the Temple, these pillars weep. Rabbi Eliezer, a son of Rabbi Yossi, says that he also saw the golden plate from the crown of the high priest preserved in Rome. On it were these identifying words: "Holiness unto the Lord."

Other legends say that the vessels were taken to the east. Some say that they were hidden in a tower in the walled city of Baghdad, others say that they were deposited in the walls of Babylon, or in the Tell Beruk under the great willow tree.

Whatever the ultimate disposition of the holy vessels may

have been, Joel declared that the Day of the Lord will finally come upon the nations for their plunder of these treasures and their desecration of the Temple.

Joel also indicated that the epicenter of the Day of the Lord will be around Jerusalem.

> I will gather all nations, and will bring them down into the valley of Jehoshaphat; and I will execute judgment upon them there. Let the nations bestir themselves, and come up to the valley of Jehoshaphat; for there will I sit to judge all the nations round about. Multitudes, multitudes in the valley of decision! For the day of the LORD is near in the valley of decision (3:2, 12, 14).

The name Jehoshaphat is composed of two Hebrew words. "Jeho" means "the LORD," while the other means "judges." The valley of Jehoshaphat is the place of divine judgment. From the time of Eusebius, who died in approximately A.D. 339, the valley of Jehoshaphat has been located in the depression called Kidron, between the Temple Mount and the Mount of Olives. Wherever it might be located, and this tradition may have substance, the valley represents the place where God's final judgment against the nations will take place. Though the valley's geography may be an open question, it is certain that it is located near Jerusalem. Here, in "the city of peace," the final confrontation between the God of Israel and the Gentile nations will transpire. The prophet said,

> Proclaim ye this among the nations; prepare war; stir up the mighty men; let all the men of war draw near, let them come up. Beat your plowshares into swords, and your pruning-hooks into spears: let the weak say, I am strong. Haste ye, and come, all ye nations round about, and gather yourselves together: thither cause thy mighty ones to come down, O LORD (3:9-11).

Here Isaiah's and Micah's great figures of peace (Is 2:4; Mic 4:3) are reversed. The beating of the swords into plowshares and the spears into pruning hooks must wait until the Messianic reign of the Lord Jesus Christ after this final battle is concluded. But first, Joel said, it will be time for the nations to be gathered around Jerusalem, for there this final conflict must occur.

The Lord's opposition to the nations on that day, and His protection of Israel is expressed by the prophet Joel who said,

> The sun and the moon are darkened, and the stars withdraw their shining. And the LORD will roar from Zion, and utter his voice from Jerusalem; and the heavens and the earth shall shake: but the LORD will be a refuge unto his people, and a stronghold to the children of Israel (3:15-16).

Jesus saw this same day, and described it in similar apocalyptic terms.

> But immediately after the tribulation of those days the sun shall be darkened, and the moon shall not give her light, and the stars shall fall from heaven, and the powers of the heavens shall be shaken: and then shall appear the sign of the Son of man in heaven: and then shall all the tribes of the earth mourn, and they shall see the Son of man coming on the clouds of heaven with power and great glory. And he shall send forth his angels with a great sound of a trumpet, and they shall gather together his elect from the four winds, from one end of heaven to the other (Mt 24:29-31).

Both Joel and Jesus had in view the Battle of Armageddon, which will culminate in the vicinity of Jerusalem, though it will begin in the north on the plain of Esdraelon beneath the ancient fortress of Megiddo. At first the nations will be contending with each other. The belligerents will be the forces of the Antichrist, which constitute the revived Roman Empire. They will contend with the "kings that come from the sunrising," the Orient (Rev 16:12-16). But when the covenant people of God are threatened by this conflagration, "The LORD will roar from Zion," said Joel.

Zechariah saw this same event and said,

> In that day shall the LORD defend the inhabitants of
> Jerusalem; and he that is feeble among them at that day
> shall be as David; and the house of David shall be as God,
> as the angel of the LORD before them. And it shall come to
> pass in that day, that I will seek to destroy all the nations
> that come against Jerusalem (12:8-9).
>
> Behold, a day of the LORD cometh, when thy spoil shall be
> divided in the midst of thee. For I will gather all nations
> against Jerusalem to battle; . . . Then shall the LORD go
> forth, and fight against those nations, as when he fought in
> the day of battle. And his feet shall stand in that day upon
> the mount of Olives, which is before Jerusalem on the east
> (14:1-4).

On the isle of Patmos, John, the aged apostle, saw this hour
and its climax, saying,

> I saw the heaven opened; and behold, a white horse, and
> he that sat thereon called Faithful and True; and in right-
> eousness he doth judge and make war. And his eyes are a
> flame of fire, and upon his head are many diadems; and he
> hath a name written which no one knoweth but he himself.
> And he is arrayed in a garment sprinkled with blood: and
> his name is called The Word of God. And the armies which
> are in heaven followed him upon white horses, clothed in
> fine linen, white and pure. And out of his mouth proceedeth
> a sharp sword, that with it he should smite the nations: and
> he shall rule them with a rod of iron: and he treadeth the
> winepress of the fierceness of the wrath of God, the Almighty.
> And he hath on his garment and on his thigh a name
> written, KING OF KINGS, AND LORD OF LORDS (Rev
> 19:11-16).

The Day of the Lord will finally have come upon the nations!

Contending with each other, the nations will have desecrated the Holy Land and threatened the covenant people of

God for the last time. The Lord will roar from Zion. The nations will be defeated. The Lord Jesus, Israel's Messiah-King, will then set up His throne in the liberated city of Jerusalem. From there He will rule the nations with a rod of iron. "So shall ye know that I am the LORD your God, dwelling in Zion my holy mountain: then shall Jerusalem be holy, and there shall no strangers pass through here any more" (Joel 3:17).

6

THE AGE OF BLESSING AFTER THE DAY OF THE LORD

Joel 3:18-21

THERE WILL BE a blessing phase of the Day of the Lord which will follow the judgment phase of that day. The nations and apostate Israel will be judged. The faithful remnant in Israel who survive the Great Tribulation period and the Battle of Armageddon will be ushered into the golden age, for they will have accepted Jesus Christ as Messiah and Saviour.

Leon Uris's novel *Exodus* dramatizes the plight of the European Jew who survived the Nazi holocaust. In his book, the novelist portrays the attitude of the Jew who contemplates the return to Eretz Israel, the land of Israel. He pictures the orthodox Messianic outlook of the older Jew in contrast to the militancy of a new generation of Jews who view the Messianic hope only in terms of Zionistic self-deliverance.

The traditional longing of the orthodox Jew is represented by Simon Rabinsky who lived in Russia. Simon was an impoverished boot-maker who struggled against the anti-Jewish society of the late nineteenth century in order to maintain himself, his wife, Rachel, and his two sons, Yakov and Jossi. Simon was finally killed during a pogrom.

On the Sabbath every ghetto Jew found release from the harsh society in which he was forced to exist. He was momentarily fulfilled as his ancient faith transported him back to the land to live out the hours between the lighting of the candles on Friday evening until sunset on Saturday among the people of ancient Israel. But with sunset the Sabbath ended and the spirit of the observant Jew returned to the ghetto. "With the day over he returned to the realities of his bitter life," says Leon Uris of Simon Rabinsky.

> In the dingy cellar he called home and shop, Simon Rabinsky would crouch over his work bench in the candle light, with his wrinkled hands drive a knife deftly through leather. Simon then said the same lament that had been said by Jews since their captivity in Babylon. . . . "If I forget thee, O Jerusalem, let my right hand forget her cunning . . . let my tongue cleave to the roof of my mouth, if I prefer not Jerusalem above my chief joy." There was solace in prayer, and Simon Rabinsky was a believer among men. But even one so devout could not shut his eyes to the misery around and above him. "How long must we live in this abysmal darkness?" And then his heart would grow light and he would become exalted as he repeated his favorite passage of the Passover Prayer—"Next year in Jerusalem." Next year in Jerusalem? Would it ever come? Would the Messiah ever come to take them back?*

Simon believed that the day would come. But that was in 1884.

After World War I and the world's manifest indifference to the plight of European Jewry during the Nazi holocaust, the attitude of many Jews changed from hope to despair, even to cynicism. Uris dramatizes the attitude of the modern Zionist in a scene set in the midst of a displaced persons camp on the isle of Cyprus just after World War II. In those days before the United Nations had partitioned Palestine in order to create the new State of Israel, Jews were still being turned away from the land by the British. From 1945 until 1947, the fate of thousands of Jewish refugees was in doubt.

*From EXODUS, by Leon Uris. Copyright © 1958 by Leon M. Uris. Used by permission.

In the center of this refugee camp there was a tent in which an improvised synagogue was set up. Above the door a crudely made Menorah was hung, giving evidence of what transpired within. Inside the tent synagogue an old man swayed back and forth as he recited Hebrew prayers. He wept and cried aloud in anguish. He told God about his life of faithfulness to the holy Torah. He had kept the commandments amid the unbelievable hardships of the Nazi holocaust. Now he asked for deliverance and for solace in the land of Israel. The pathos of this scene was abruptly broken as Uris contrasted the outlook of the older Jew with that of the new generation. A young Jew remarked. "The old man in there doesn't quite realize that the only Messiah that will deliver [the Jews] is a bayonet on the end of a rifle!"[1]

Joel predicted deliverance such as Simon Rabinsky prayed for. But it will not be the kind of deliverance which this youthful and caustic Jewish militant in *Exodus* envisioned it to be. The Day of the Lord will yet deliver Israel, in spite of centuries of delay which have caused the reinterpretation of the Jewish Messianic hope and even its complete abandonment by many modern Jews.

Usually the full title "The Day of the Lord" is used by the prophets to designate the coming judgment upon the nations which will issue in the deliverance of Israel.

However, the Hebrew prophets often designated the Day of the Lord as simply "that day." So significant is "that day" that no other modifiers are needed in the prophet's language to give sufficient impetus to his pronouncements about the judgment upon the nations, or blessings upon Israel, which are to come in "that day."

Zechariah, for example, said,

> And it shall come to pass in *that day*, that I will make Jerusalem a burdensome stone for all the peoples (12:3).
>
> In *that day*, saith the Lord, I will smite every horse with terror, and his rider with madness (12:4).

> In *that day* will I make the chieftains of Judah like a pan
> of fire among the wood (12:6).
>
> In *that day* shall the Lord defend the inhabitants of Jeru-
> salem; and he that is feeble among them at *that day* shall be
> as David (12:8).
>
> And it shall come to pass in *that day,* that I will seek to
> destroy all the nations that come against Jerusalem (12:9).
>
> In *that day* shall there be a great mourning in Jerusalem
> (12:11, italics added).

"That day" will be a day of judgment upon the nations.
"That day" will also be a day of blessing for Israel.
Zechariah said,

> In *that day* there shall be a fountain opened to the house
> of David and to the inhabitants of Jerusalem, for sin and
> for uncleanness. And it shall come to pass in *that day,* saith
> the Lord of hosts, that I will cut off the names of the idols
> out of the land, and they shall no more be remembered; and
> also I will cause the prophets and the unclean spirit to pass
> out of the land (13:1-2, italics added).

Joel also used "that day" in a similar manner. It will be a
day of judgment, but it will also be a day of blessing to come
upon Israel when the Day of the Lord ushers in the Messianic
age. Though Joel did not, at that early date, see a personal
Messiah, he did forecast the blessing of the Messianic age
which will follow the judgment phase of the Day of the Lord
(the Great Tribulation period and the second coming of
Christ). As Joel brought his prophecy to a close, having predicted judgment upon the nations, he said, "And it shall come
to pass in that day," and then he enumerated four blessings
which the covenant people of God are to receive (3:18-21).
These blessings are: (1) the healing of the land (v. 18); (2)
the obliteration of all of Israel's enemies (v. 19); (3) a se-
curing of the land for all future times (v. 20); and (4) the
vindication of Israel as God's chosen people, for the Lord
will come to dwell among them in Zion (v. 21).

"That day" will be a day of healing for the land.

Amos concluded his prophecy, as did Joel, by saying,

> In that day will I raise up the tabernacle of David that is
> fallen, and close up the breaches thereof; and I will raise up
> its ruins, and I will build it as in the days of old; that they
> may possess the remnant of Edom, and all the nations that
> are called by my name, saith the LORD that doeth this. Be-
> hold, the days come, saith the LORD, that the plowman shall
> overtake the reaper, and the treader of grapes him that
> soweth seed; and the mountains shall drop sweet wine, and
> all the hills shall melt. And I will bring back the captivity
> of my people Israel, and they shall build the waste cities,
> and inhabit them; and they shall plant vineyards, and drink
> the wine thereof; they shall also make gardens, and eat the
> fruit of them. And I will plant them upon their land, and
> they shall no more be plucked up out of their land which I
> have given them, saith the LORD thy God (Amos 9:11-15).

Joel put it this way:

> And it shall come to pass in that day, that the mountains
> shall drop down sweet wine, and the hills shall flow with
> milk, and all the brooks of Judah shall flow with waters; and
> a fountain shall come forth from the house of the LORD, and
> shall water the valley of Shittim (3:18).

The ecological balance between the physical and the spiritual world has already been noted. When evil prevails, the
physical earth suffers. When righteousness reigns, as it will
in the Messianic age, then the earth benefits by this environment. Most of the Hebrew prophets envisioned the time
when the earth will be healed of sin's primal curse. Both
Amos and Joel presented a picture of the Messianic age in
which the physical curse of sin will be removed and the Messiah's reign of righteousness will bring healing to the land.

Joel's imagery depicts the land fluid with liquid luxury.
We must recall that Joel was living in the time of the locust

plague. His country had been ravished by the incursion of devouring locusts. The land was stripped bare. In addition, a mighty drought was raging even as he preached.

> For the fire hath devoured the pastures of the wilderness, and the flame hath burned all the trees of the field. Yea, the beasts of the field pant unto thee; for the water brooks are dried up, and the fire hath devoured the pastures of the wilderness (1:19-20).

This is what his physical eyes saw as he looked about. However, Joel's spiritual eyes saw something else. While predicting the Day of the Lord and the Messianic age which will follow, Joel also saw the landscape of Eretz Israel transformed by flowing streams.

There will be rivulets, for the brooks of Judah will emanate with fresh, cool, sparkling water.

But the prophet saw even more.

Down the mountainside will flow streams of sweet wine, while the hillsides will run with rills of milk. Not only will the streams of Judah never dry up again, as they had in the drought of Joel's day, but they will pour down a variety of liquids—water, wine, and milk! Joel's hyperboles emphasize both the quantity and quality of the physical blessings which will follow the Messianic transformation of the land.

If the streams of wine and milk are hyperboles of extreme fertility, is the "fountain [which] shall come forth from the house of the LORD, and shall water the valley of Shittim" also a figure of speech?

Perhaps. However, both the prophets Ezekiel (47:1-12) and Zechariah (14:8) apparently saw a similar issue of water from the Temple area. All three of these prophets, Joel, Ezekiel, and Zechariah, seem to confirm the reality of this stream which will exist during the Messianic age and will flow from Jerusalem down to the Dead Sea.

Ezekiel said, "And, behold, waters issued out from under

the threshold of the house eastward; [for the forefront of the house was toward the east;] and the waters came down from under, from the right side of the house, on the south of the altar" (Eze 47:1). As the prophet Ezekiel and his angelic companion followed the stream, crisscrossing it every so often, they found that it grew progressively deeper—ankle deep (47:3), knee deep, waist deep (47:4)—and finally, they had to swim across it for it was over their heads (47:5). Along its banks grew trees (47:7). These were a type of

> tree for food, whose leaf shall not wither, neither shall the fruit thereof fail: it shall bring forth new fruit every month, because the waters thereof issue out of the sanctuary; and the fruit thereof shall be for food, and the leaf thereof for healing (47:12).

This river ultimately will flow into the Dead Sea whose waters are healed of brackishess. The Dead Sea will then teem with aquatic life (47:9-10).

The prophet Zechariah added a second dimension to this river which will flow during the Messianic age. He declared that "it shall come to pass in that day, that living waters shall go out from Jerusalem; half of them toward the eastern sea, and half of them toward the western sea: in summer and in winter shall it be" (Zec 14:8). Both Ezekiel and Zechariah said that the Dead Sea, "the eastern sea," will receive the healing waters of this river. Zechariah added that the Mediterranean Sea, "the western sea," will also benefit by it.

The words of these two prophets encourages us to treat these words of Joel literally: "And a fountain shall come forth from the house of the LORD, and shall water the valley of Shittim" (3:18).

Shittim is the name of the last encampment of the Exodus, just before the Hebrew people entered the land (Num 25:1; Jos 3:1). It is unlikely that Joel would picture the stream intersecting the Jordan and then fertilizing the bank on the opposite side. We must look elsewhere for the location of the valley of Shittim.

The Hebrew word for "valley" corresponds to the Arabic word *wady*. Most students of Joel identify the *wady* of Shittim with the Kidron Valley which lies along the eastern side of the old city of Jerusalem between Temple Mount and the Mount of Olives. Beginning northwest of Jerusalem, this depression runs in a southeasterly direction, past the city, until it reaches the Dead Sea. This is the same valley down which Ezekiel's river is to flow.

Shittim is the name of the wood which comes from the acacia tree. The point here is that the acacia tree grows in very dry soil. In the future this valley will no longer be dry, supporting little more than the acacia tree, but it will become fertile as it is watered by this perennial stream issuing from the Temple.

The rabbis have a tradition that the waters of this stream will wash away the debris which conceals the lost vessels of the Temple. These sacred vessels will be restored to use when the stream reveals them.

Joel, along with others of the Hebrew prophets, used vivid language containing dramatic imagery to describe the transformation of the land during the Messianic age. However, the substance of what he said seems to be real rather than ideal. While creeks of wine and milk may symbolize the fertility of the renewed land, the stream which issues from the Temple should be taken both seriously and literally. This phenomena of the Messianic age finds much confirmation in other Scripture.

Joel, by his luxurious language, was affirming the richness of the transformed land of Israel after the devastation of the Day of the Lord. His language conveys a thrilling anticipation of the land restored to its milk and honey state, and beyond, to the state of ideal fertility. The prophets always view Israel's golden age as yet future. It is not in a remote past which can only be remembered as a zenith of affluence from which the people have fallen. Unlike the Greeks, the Jews look forward to a time of restoration in which the ideal world is to be realized in the Messiah's reign. All these predictions are to be fulfilled when the second coming of Christ transforms this physical realm, which has been rendered chaotic by sin, into the millennial earth with all of its dramatic renovations, both physical and spiritual.

"That day" will also spell the end of Israel's enemies. "Egypt shall be a desolation, and Edom shall be a desolate wilderness, for the violence done to the children of Judah, because they have shed innocent blood in their land," said Joel (3:19).

Egypt and Edom are the traditional enemies of Israel. Their demise symbolizes the end of all hostility and anti-Semitism. At long last the Jew will be at peace with all people.

Here Joel indicated the end of the Arab-Israeli conflict.

This particular hostility goes far back into history, much farther back than does the persecution of the Jew for merely religious or cultural reasons. In fact, religious persecution did not occur in history until the second century B.C. when Antiochus IV Epiphanes persecuted the Jews because they would not accept Hellenism as a religion and a way of life. The conflict between the Jew and the Arab dates back 4,000 years to the hostility between Isaac and Ishmael. This particular antagonism was divinely forecast in the Torah. The angel of the Lord said to Hagar,

> Behold, thou art with child, and shalt bear a son; and thou shalt call his name Ishmael, because the LORD hath heard thy affliction. And he shall be as a wild ass among men; his hand shall be against every man, and every man's hand against him; and he shall dwell over against all of his brethren (Gen 16:11-12).

The Arab people are the descendants of Ishmael. The

Edomites, of whom Joel also spoke, are descendants of Esau, the brother of Jacob and the son of Isaac. They too are Arabs. But they are also the special enemies of Israel. To Rebekah, Esau's mother, God said, "Two nations are in thy womb, and two peoples shall be separated from thy bowels: and the one people shall be stronger than the other people; and the elder shall serve the younger" (Gen 25:23). The Edomites epitomized the enemies of God's covenant people Israel. In the Talmud and the Midrash the rabbis even refer to Rome, Israel's greatest enemy and persecutor in the ancient world, as "Edom."

Joel not only predicted the end of the Arab-Israeli conflict, but he also predicted the end of the worldwide psychosis of anti-Semitism.

Anti-Semitism was a fact of life for the Jews in the ancient world. Cicero, the Roman Stoic who lived in the century preceding the birth of Christ, said that it was evident "how much the immortal gods abhor this nation [the Jews] from the fact that it has been conquered, heavily taxed, and beaten to the ground." Two thousand years have not substantially altered the attitude of the Gentile world toward the Jew. The twentieth century has seen the worst Jewish persecution in history when the Nazis attempted genocide as the ultimate expression of this anti-Semitism.

A word in the English language refers almost exclusively to Jewish persecutions. It is *pogrom,* a word which comes from the Russian language. It means "devastation" in Russian and is defined as "an organized massacre of helpless people, especially the Jewish people." On March 3, 1881, Alexander II, Czar of Russia, was killed by a bomb. The Jews were implicated. A cry went up all across Russia, "Kill the Jews who killed our Lord Jesus and our little father, the Czar!" The pogroms began on Easter Sunday, 1881, as the Russian people massacred thousands of Jews, to the accompaniment of ringing church bells. Jews who were not killed or maimed attempted to flee Russia. Those who could not flee suffered intolerably under the May Laws which, from 1882, permitted no Jew to take residence in any Russian village except by special and costly dispensation.

However, these Russian pogroms were only a prelude to a much more horrible persecution of the Jews which erupted a half century later in Hitler's Germany. Like the word *pogrom,* the term *the Holocaust* is used when referring exclusively to the Nazis' murder of six million Jews and to the Jewish remnant which managed to survive Hitler's final solution to the Jewish problem, genocide.

The ancient rabbis believed that the burning bush, out of which God spoke to Moses, was a symbol of the nation Israel. Just as the bush was unconsumed by the flames, so Israel will not be consumed by her enemies. In the Midrash the rabbis observed that the word for "bush" occurs four times in Exodus 3:2. This, said the rabbis, signifies these four exiles which Israel has experienced at the hands of her enemies: the exile in Egypt, the one in Babylon, the exile under the Greeks when Antiochus IV Epiphanes attempted to force Hellenism upon the Jews (a spiritual exile according to the rabbis), and the final exile when the Romans destroyed the second Temple. The bush survived the fire, so the sages also declared that Israel would survive these four exiles and overcome her enemies.

The Midrashic rabbis saw an additional symbol in this bush. The thorn bush releases no bird which alights in its branches, they said, without lacerating that bird's wings. So none of the nations which have subjugated Israel will escape punishment.

With this Joel concurred.

The enemies of God's covenant people Israel, symbolized by Egypt and Edom, will finally be subdued. Egypt shall be a desolation. Edom will become a desolate wilderness.

Joel's third prediction about the aftermath of the Day of the Lord was that Israel will be secured in the land forevermore. "But Judah shall abide forever, and Jerusalem from generation to generation" (3:20).

Why is security in the land so important to the Hebrew people?

The physical existence of the Jew in the land is an indispensable ingredient in the Jewish ethos. For the last 2,000 years the Jew has lived in exile. During this time he created a sort of portable homeland through the Talmud. This kept the Jew intact during all these years. No other nation in history has been dispersed among other nations without becoming assimilated, resulting in a total loss of self-identity. But not the Jew. He has retained, even in exile, a self-conscious identity. There are other reasons for this persistence besides the Talmud. The Hebrew language, his kosher practices, his Sabbath observances, his synagogue services, the ghetto—all have united to keep the Jew distinct. By these he has held his own against the tides of assimilation. Of course, behind all of this are God's divine purposes for Israel which have maintained the Jew during the course of his history.

However, in this economic, political, and spiritual isolation, the Jew's creative genius was slowly atrophying. It was the dynamic of Zionism during the last century which saved the Jew from shriveling away in the cocoon of ghetto civilization. The renewal of interest in the homeland gave a new incentive to the creative power of the people. The release of Zionism provided a new scope to the Jew's spiritual creativity. Today the State of Israel, a miracle of political, social, and economic creativity, is the medium of the Jew's new vitality.

During the glorious age to come, the nation in the land will also be the context of a new spiritual civilization. For regenerated Israel under the Messiah's reign will experience all the spiritual potential which is included in Jeremiah's forecast of the new covenant (Jer 31:31-34; cf. Eze 36:24-28).

We now see that only in the land is the Jew truly aggressive in his creativity. Outside the land he improvises for survival, but inside the land his genius is freed for progress.

This is an innate quality of Jewishness.

In his *Memoirs,* David Ben Gurion wrote,

> The uniqueness of the Jewish people and of Judaism consists in this: no other religion is connected with the physical existence of the nation. Remove Jewish history and there is no Judaism. This explains our attachment to Israel. And to my mind it accounts for the fact that if the Bible stresses creativity, the Jews not as individuals but as Jews were, and only are, truly creative when living in their own land.[2]

Joel said that the day is coming when this dynamic of Jewishness will have full release in the security of the homeland.

The Messiah, the Lord Jesus Christ, whom the Jews will accept as Saviour and Lord at His second coming, will establish a reign upon this earth which will issue in peace and security for all people. It will also become the context in which the nation Israel will realize the golden age which her ancient prophets predicted.

Who can anticipate what the creative genius of the Jew, under the lordship of Jesus Christ, will produce during the Messianic era which is yet to come? Within the security of the land, redeemed Israel will become a blessing for all mankind, fulfilling at long last God's elective purposes for which He long ago chose the nation. Released from spiritual blindness and transformed by the new birth, Israel will dwell in the land, untrammeled by hostile neighbors. Here is the matrix for a unique spiritual civilization over which the Messiah will reign. Out of this new spiritual culture will come the social order for which mankind has always longed and toward which humanity has feebly striven. Israel, spiritually regenerated and dwelling safely in the land, will be the medium for disseminating this new spiritual culture to all the redeemed of the millennial earth. It is then that Joel's imagery, "plowshares into swords" and "pruning-hooks into spears" (3: 10), will be reversed. "And they shall beat their swords into plowshares, and their spears into pruning-hooks; nation shall not lift up sword against nation, neither shall they learn war any more" (Is 2:4; Mic 4:3).

"And I will cleanse their blood, that I have not cleansed: for the LORD dwelleth in Zion" (Joel 3:21).

Joel predicted a fourth feature of the Messianic age. It will be the Lord's vindication of His people Israel. The meaning of Joel's prophetic declaration is clarified in the Revised Version margin. It reads, "And I will hold [declare] as innocent their blood which I have not held innocent." Israel has suffered at the hands of the Egyptians and the Edomites, who actually represent all the enemies and oppressors of Israel. Now the Lord will justify His people.

Have the Jews deserved all the suffering which they have endured through these many years? God's inaction on Israel's behalf might indicate that this is the case. But at long last, the Lord will clear His people from suspicion in two ways, for He will not only punish Israel's enemies, but He Himself will come to live in Zion among His people.

Israel's enemies have shed innocent blood. Therefore when Egypt becomes a desolation and Edom a desolate wilderness, Israel will be exonerated. This will demonstrate that God has not forsaken His people.

However, the Lord's presence will be actual among them, for, "the LORD dwelleth in Zion." The book of Joel opens with the pessimistic picture of Israel forsaken and subject to the ravages of the locust plague and drought. It closes with the optimistic affirmation that the Lord is with them, dwelling in Zion.

Joel's words "the LORD dwelleth in Zion" represent the fulfillment of Israel's longing because this is the ultimate expression of the Zionist aspiration: Israel in the land and the LORD in her midst, "dwelling in Zion!"

The Jews have done what is humanly possible to implement these aspirations of Zionism.

From 1948 they have literally fought for the land while living in the land. This has not happened since the last Jewish defense of the land way back in A.D. 135 when the Jews rebelled against the Romans for the last time. But now, to quote Dimont, "From the attic of their history the Jews had taken down the shield of David and the armor of Bar Kokhba. Once again they were marching under Jewish generals giving commands in Hebrew."[3] Four wars had erupted by the time Israel celebrated her silver anniversary—the War of Independence in 1948; the Sinai campaign of 1956; the 1967 Six Day War; and the Yom Kippur War of 1973. Yet the State of Israel persists against what seems to be insurmountable odds. The Jews are in the land to stay. They are determined never again to become exiles and refugees. They are prepared not only to fight but also to die for the right to a homeland.

Today Zionism has a military posture.

But for the first fifty years of its history, Zionism's initiative was an idealism which would be expressed in purely intellectual terms, followed by an era of political intrigue.

Between 1860 and 1900 the Zionists wrote emancipation books and pamphlets in which they proposed various solutions to the Jewish national problem. In 1862 Moses Hess wrote *Rome and Jerusalem* in which he advocated a return of the Jews to Palestine to create a spiritual center for Diaspora Judaism. Hess was the philosopher of Zionism. Peretz Smolenskin represented an intellectualized Zionism. Writing in a pamphlet called *The Eternal People,* Smolenskin declared that the Jews were an intellectual people held together by the Hebrew language, but needing a homeland in order that Jewish genius might flourish, much like David Ben Gurion's thesis. Leo Pinsker deplored current assimilationist answers to the Jewish dilemma and advocated territorial independence for the Jew in his famous *Auto-Emancipation.* Only a home base could save the Jews from the threat of destruction due to the worldwide psychosis of anti-Semitism.

It was Theodor Herzl who finally personified the Zionist aspiration when he became convinced, through witnessing the Dreyfus trial, that the Jew lived in an innately hostile world and can survive neither ghetto isolationism nor assimilation. He wrote *The Jewish State,* which was published in 1896. Herzl diverted the Messianic ideal of Judaism from spiritual into political channels. At the first Zionist Congress, held in Basel in 1897, Herzl predicted that an independent state of Israel would be in existence within fifty years.

His prediction failed by nine months!

These early Zionist intellectuals persuaded 115,000 Jews to return to Palestine before World War I. In 1917 Zionism was given a political turn by the Balfour Declaration which said, "His Majesty's Government views with favour the establishment in Palestine of a national home for the Jewish people." What Lord Balfour set forth in his famous letter as the official British attitude toward the question of a Jewish homeland, the British government denied in action. They made a secret deal with the Arabs, promising them concessions of land in the Middle East if they would revolt against the Turks. Though unspecified, the Arabs assumed that Palestine was included in this agreement. The British later issued a white paper in which Jewish immigration into Palestine was severely curtailed. It was against British political opposition that Zionism attempted to maneuver during the day of the British Mandate. The British attitude was generally pro-Arab.

Success came after World War II.

Zionism lost many battles with the British; however, the Zionist war was won when the British were forced to hand the problem of the mandate over to the United Nations in 1947. This world body proposed a solution to the Jewish problem by voting a partition of Palestine. There would be two states, one Arab and the other the new state of Israel, so they decreed. The partition of Palestine was realized on May 15, 1948. Immediately the Arab legions attacked Israel, and the military phase of Zionism was begun.

It continues today.

Zionism's rationale, which was, in turn, intellectual, political, and military, helped to create and to maintain the present State of Israel.

And today Jews continue to return to the land.

Yet, they are returning in unbelief.

Philosophical, political, and militant Zionism must yet be followed by a spiritual Zionism. This is the theme of Joel's closing prophecy, for he predicted that the time will come when the Lord will dwell in Zion amid His people Israel. When Joel's prophecy comes to pass, then the fulfillment of the Zionist aspiration will be fully manifest.

Zionism was conceived by Jewish intellectuals and philosophers.

It was implemented by Jewish political activists.

It is propelled by Jewish militants in the land today.

However, one day God Himself must fulfill the Zionist prospect with a great spiritual revolution if the vision of Joel, along with the other Hebrew prophets, is to be realized.

The modern State of Israel came into existence on the fifth day of Iyar in the year 5708, according to the Jewish calendar. On our calendar it was the Sabbath eve, May 14, 1948, when Israel's first prime minister, David Ben Gurion, stood before the portrait of Herzl in the Tel Aviv Museum and read the formal Proclamation of Independence:

> In the Land of Israel the Jewish people came into being. In this Land was shaped their spiritual, religious and national character. Here they lived in sovereign independence. Here they created a culture of national and universal import, and gave to the world the eternal Book of Books.
>
> Exiled by force, still the Jewish people kept faith with

the Land in all the countries of their dispersion, steadfast in their prayers and hope to return and here revive their political freedom.

Fired by this attachment of history and tradition the Jews in every generation strove to renew their roots in the ancient Homeland.

Ben Gurion's reading was interrupted just once. When he read the words, "The State of Israel will be open to Jewish immigration and the ingathering of the exiles," wild applause broke the solemnity of the occasion.

Ben Gurion added, the State of Israel "will rest upon the foundations of liberty, justice and peace as envisioned by the Prophets of Israel."

And so it does, to the extent that the governing capacity of man can implement the ideals of the prophets.

And yet, the contemporary State of Israel is far from what the prophets actually forecast. For what the prophets of Israel, Joel included, predicted can be realized only by divine intervention into history.

Intellectual, political, and militant Zionism has helped to set the stage. The people are returning to the land as never before. The State of Israel stands upon the eastern shore of the Mediterranean. For the first time in nearly 2,000 years the Jews have a homeland in Eretz Israel.

Yet the ideal and spiritual dimensions of the prophet's visions have not been realized. The dry bones have assembled, but as yet there is no spirit in them.

But the day is coming!

> Then he said unto me, Son of man, these bones are the whole house of Israel: behold, they say, Our bones are dried up, and our hope is lost; we are clean cut off. Therefore prophesy, and say unto them, Thus saith the LORD God: Behold, I will open your graves, and cause you to come up out of your graves, O my people; and I will bring you into the land of Israel. And ye shall know that I am the LORD,

> when I have opened your graves, and caused you to come up
> out of your graves, O my people. And I will put my Spirit
> in you, and ye shall live, and I will place you in your own
> land: and ye shall know that I, the LORD, have spoken it and
> performed it, saith the LORD (Eze 37:11-14).

When will this final phase of spiritual Zionism, which the
prophet Ezekiel envisioned, be realized? He declared,

> Thus saith the LORD God: I will gather you from the
> peoples, and assemble you out of the countries where ye
> have been scattered, and I will give you the land of Israel.
> And I will give them one heart, and I will put a new spirit
> within you; and I will take the stony heart out of their flesh,
> and will give them a heart of flesh; that they may walk in
> my statutes, and keep mine ordinances, and do them: and
> they shall be my people, and I will be their God (Eze 11:
> 17, 19-20).

But there must be a catalyst for all this.

What produces the spiritual transformation of the people
who have been gathered back to the land in unbelief?

It is the second coming of Christ.

"Behold, he cometh with the clouds; and every eye shall see
him, and they that pierced him; and all the tribes of the earth
shall mourn over him. Even so, Amen" (Rev 1:7).

> And I will pour upon the house of David, and upon the
> inhabitants of Jerusalem, the spirit of grace and of supplica-
> tion; and they shall look unto me whom they have pierced;
> and they shall mourn for him, as one mourneth for his only
> son, and shall be in bitterness for him, as one that is in
> bitterness for his first-born. In that day there shall be a
> fountain opened to the house of David and to the inhabi-
> tants of Jerusalem, for sin and for uncleanness" (Zec 12:10;
> 13:1).

In that day, when Jesus comes a second time, the Jews will
receive Him as Messiah and Saviour.

Then the golden age of the Messiah's reign will be ushered in. Then will be fulfilled all that Joel, along with the rest of the Hebrew prophets, predicted for Israel.

NOTES

Chapter 1

1. S. R. Driver, *The Books of Joel and Amos,* The Cambridge Bible for Schools and Colleges (Cambridge: U. Press, 1915), pp. 19-22.
2. R. F. Horton, *The Minor Prophets,* The Century Bible (Edinburgh: T. & T. Clark, n.d.), 1:82-83.
3. J. Barton Payne, *Encyclopedia of Biblical Prophecy* (New York: Harper & Row, 1973), p. 407.
4. Frederick Carl Eiselein, *The Minor Prophets* (New York: Eaton & Mains, 1907), p. 148.
5. John R. Sampey, *The Heart of the Old Testament* (Nashville: Broadman, 1922), p. 148.
6. H. H. Rowley, *The Faith of Israel* (Philadelphia: Westminster, 1956), pp. 178-79. Used by permission.

Chapter 2

1. W. M. Thomson, *The Land and the Book* (New York: Harper, 1876), 2:102-6.
2. William H. Townsend, *Lincoln and the Bluegrass* (Lexington, Ky.: U. Kentucky, 1955), pp. 97-98.
3. C. F. Keil, *The Twelve Minor Prophets* (Grand Rapids: Eerdmans, 1949), 1:184.
4. Julius Bewer, *Obadiah and Joel,* The International Critical Commentary (Edinburgh: T. & T. Clark, 1912), p. 78.
5. Thomson, p. 105.
6. Josephus *Antiquities* 14. 4. 3. Cf. Abraham Rabinovich, "1900th Anniversary of the Destruction," *Israel Magazine* 3, no. 3 (Mar. 1971): 57.
7. Josephus *Wars* 5. 12. 3.
8. John D. Whiting, "Jerusalem's Locust Plague," *National Geographic* 28, no. 6 (Dec. 1915): 513.
9. S. Hieronymi, *Presbyteri Opera,* Commentarii in Prophetas Minores (Turnholti: Typographi Brepols Editors Pontificii, 1969), 76, PARS I, 6, p. 163.
10. A. Cohen, ed., *The Twelve Prophets,* The Soncino Books of the Bible (London: Soncino, 1969), p. 58.
11. Whiting, p. 535.
12. Ibid., p. 513.
13. David A. Hubbard, "Joel," *Christianity Today,* June 9, 1958, pp. 23, 38. Copyright 1958 by *Christianity Today.* Used by permission.

CHAPTER 3

1. John A. Broadus, *Commentary on the Gospel of Matthew* (Philadelphia: Amer. Bap. Pub. Soc., 1886), p. 51.
2. *Midrash on the Psalms,* 22.5.
3. H. C. O. Lancaster, *The Books of Joel and Amos,* The Cambridge Bible for Schools and Colleges (Cambridge: U. Press, 1915), p. 56.

CHAPTER 4

1. *Talmud,* Yoma 86.
2. *Tanhuma Yashan K'doshim,* 38.
3. *Pirke De Rabbi Eliezer,* chap. 18.
4. John D. Whiting, "Jerusalem's Locust Plague," *National Geographic* 28, no. 6 (Dec. 1915): 513.
5. Frederick Carl Eiselein, *The Minor Prophets* (New York: Eaton & Mains, 1907), p. 177.
6. *The Midrash on Psalms,* 132. 1.
7. W. O. Carver, *The Acts of the Apostles* (Nashville: Broadman, 1916), p. 28.
8. *Talmud,* Menahot, 53.
9. *Talmud,* Nedarim, 49*b.*

CHAPTER 5

1. Thomas R. Bransten, ed., *Memoirs: David Ben Gurion* (New York: World, 1970), p. 20.
2. *Talmud,* Berakot, 3*a.*
3. *Sifre'* to Deut. 11:17.
4. *Talmud,* Sanhedrin, 37*b.*
5. Bransten, pp. 18, 38.
6. Golda Meir, *A Land of Our Own* (New York: Putnam's Sons, 1973), p. 117.
7. *Bereshit Rabbeti,* 78.
8. Nathan Ausubel, ed., *A Treasury of Jewish Folklore* (New York: Crown, 1961), p. 487. Copyright, 1948, by Crown Publishers. Used by permission of Crown Publishers, Inc.
9. H. Wheeler Robinson, *The History of Israel* (London: Duckworth, 1949), p. 98.
10. Clyde T. Francisco, *Introducing the Old Testament* (Nashville: Broadman, 1950), p. 92.
11. Josephus *Antiquities* 12. 9. 3.
12. A. Cohen, ed., *The Twelve Prophets,* The Soncino Books of the Bible (London: Soncino, 1969), p. 75.

CHAPTER 6

1. Leon Uris, *Exodus* (New York: Bantam Books, 1969), pp. 198, 56.
2. Thomas R. Bransten, ed., *Memoirs: David Ben Gurion* (New York: World, 1970), p. 20.
3. Max I. Dimont, *Jews, God, and History* (New York: Signet, 1964), p. 390.